School
Made
Easier

School Made Easier

A Kid's Guide to Study Strategies and Anxiety-Busting Tools

by Wendy L. Moss, PhD, and
Robin A. DeLuca-Acconi, LCSW

MAGINATION PRESS • WASHINGTON, DC
AMERICAN PSYCHOLOGICAL ASSOCIATION

This book is dedicated to all those who encouraged us as we wrote this book and to the students who have worked hard to overcome academic anxiety and used the study strategies to help them in school.

—WLM & RADA

Published by
MAGINATION PRESS
An Educational Publishing Foundation Book
American Psychological Association
750 First Street, NE
Washington, DC 20002

For more information about our books, including a complete catalog, please write to us, call 1-800-374-2721, or visit our website at www.apa.org/pubs/magination.

Book design by Naylor Design, Inc., Washington, DC
Printed by Worzalla, Stevens Point, WI

Library of Congress Cataloging-in-Publication Data

Moss, Wendy (Wendy L.)
    School made easier : a kid's guide to study strategies and anxiety-busting tools / by Wendy L. Moss, PhD, and Robin A. DeLuca-Acconi, LCSW.
        pages cm
    ISBN 978-1-4338-1335-1 (hardcover)—ISBN 1-4338-1335-1 (hardcover)—ISBN 978-1-4338-1336-8 (pbk.) — ISBN 1-4338-1336-X (pbk.) 1. Study skills—Juvenile literature. 2. Test anxiety—Juvenile literature. 3. Stress (Psychology)—Prevention—Juvenile literature. I. DeLuca-Acconi, Robin A. II. Title.
    LB1049.M686 2014
    371.30281—dc23
                                                                    2013005777

Manufactured in the United States of America
10 9 8 7 6 5 4 3 2 1

Contents

Note to Readers

On the first day of school, students and teachers usually have high hopes for a great year. However, as work piles on and test dates approach, a lot of kids start to feel stressed and struggle to deal with it. Does this describe you? This book is designed to help!

Congratulations on wanting to make school less stressful and more fun. As you read this book, you will hear from other kids about their feelings of stress and frustration with school work. While many kids have shared their thoughts and experiences with us, those thoughts remain private and confidential. The examples in this book are composites drawn from what we have learned from talking to kids. We hope that as you read about study strategies and anxiety-busting tools that have helped other kids, you will find some strategies that work for you.

In this book, you will learn some ways to reduce your anxiety, increase your confidence in school, and study more effectively. Believe it or not, these strategies are pretty easy to learn, and can even be fun to use!

In Chapter 1, you will learn that there are some things you can control about school and some that you can't. However, even when you can't change the pressures you are facing, you can change how you react to them. In this first chapter, you will learn to identify the signs and symptoms of stress. Once you realize that you are stressed, it's easier to find ways to cope.

In Chapters 2 and 3, you will get a crash course on how to manage academic stress by turning negative thoughts into positive self-talk, building up your confidence, and relaxing your mind and body. Also, you will read about ways to set clear and manageable goals.

After learning how to identify what causes you stress and learning how to manage it, you will learn ways to make studying less stressful. There are quick and *really* easy—we're not just saying this!—ways to get organized and start your work. In Chapters 4 and 5, you'll learn about executive functioning skills. These skills have helped adults and kids focus and get their work done. Many of these skills just take a few minutes each day to use.

When it's time to study, you may want to run, scream, or roll your eyes. Hang in there. Chapters 6 and 7 will show you some fun and effective ways to study. These suggestions have worked for other kids and they can work for you, too.

Finally, in Chapter 8 you will be coached on how to get ready for the big day when you have a test or presentation in school. You will learn some strategies to make these days not just survivable but comfortable and even, perhaps, exciting and confidence-building.

It's helpful to have another person join you as you practice the skills in this book. You may want to read this book with an adult who can support you on your journey toward managing school stress and academic pressures. You may even find that reading this book with another student can allow you both to practice the skills together.

Have fun!

—Wendy L. Moss, PhD, and Robin A. DeLuca-Acconi, LCSW

1.

Understanding Academic Stress

Do you ever get nervous about a big test? Do you get butterflies in your stomach before giving a presentation? Some kids don't mind—or even enjoy—their school work, but other kids find it stressful some of the time or even all the time. What about you? Take a minute to read the list below and figure out how much you really know about your stress. It's not a test! There aren't any right or wrong answers. You can check off all the boxes, some of them, or none.

- ☐ I know how my body feels when I'm stressed.
- ☐ I know how I behave and think when I'm stressed.
- ☐ I know some things at school and at home that make me feel stressed.
- ☐ I know how my thoughts and feelings can make me feel stressed.
- ☐ I know that stress can actually be good sometimes.

Even if you generally like school, you may find that there are times when you feel stressed. For example, Eli said, "I always liked school because I hung with my friends and I usually had nice teachers. But, I used to get really nervous when I had a test or right before the school play when I had a big role." If you find that you also feel stressed sometimes during your school day, you should know that there are strategies to help Eli, and you.

Think back to the items that you just checked off at the beginning of the chapter. How much do you know about your stress? Everyone gets stressed sometimes, and even if you checked off all of the answers, chances are you could benefit from learning new ways to handle your stress!

It's important to realize that there are some things you can control and some things you can't. Even when you can't control or change the pressures you feel at school or from schoolwork, you can change how you react to your stress.

The first thing to do is to learn how to identify when you are stressed and how your body reacts to stress. Then you can look out for the signs that you are stressed and be prepared to deal with it.

Signs and Symptoms of Stress

How do you know if you are under stress? Your body and mind send you messages. You may have experienced some of the symptoms described in this section but weren't sure why—it may have been due to stress.

TOOL KIT FOR UNDERSTANDING YOUR STRESS

- Recognize the signs and symptoms of stress by listening to what your body is telling you and paying attention to how you are acting.

- Determine the cause of your stress—is it external, internal, or both?

- Figure out if the stress you are feeling is positive stress.

Listen to Your Body

There is no one symptom of stress. The more aware you are of your body, the better you will be able to know how you react to stress or tension. Some common physical symptoms of stress include:

- fast heartbeat
- butterflies in your stomach
- headaches
- sudden change in body temperature (feeling cold or hot)
- shakiness or unsteadiness
- difficulty focusing
- nail-biting or other nervous habits
- changes in your sleep (more or less than usual)
- changes in how you eat (more or less than usual)
- fast breathing or feeling short of breath

Knowing the signs that you are stressed can help you deal with it!

There are actually good reasons why our bodies react in these ways. In the old days, our ancestors had to find a way to survive among tigers, lions, and other dangers. If they were ever in danger, they needed to have a quick energy boost to run away or fight the predator. They may even have needed to stay very still or play dead. When our bodies get ready to battle, run away, or freeze, we get a burst of energy—our heart beats faster, our breathing speeds up, and our muscles get tense. This is often called the "fight, flight, or freeze" response.

Hopefully, you never have a test that makes you feel like your life is in jeopardy and you need to fight or flee the classroom! However, our bodies automatically prepare us for stressful situations with the "fight, flight, or freeze" response, even when the stress really isn't a life-threatening danger. Carlos said, "I thought I was going crazy because I started waking up in the middle of the night with my heart beating really hard. It felt like it was trying to jump out of me. My dad took me to the doctor who checked me out. My heart was fine. It was actually talking to me. Imagine that! It was letting me know that I was really, really stressed because of mid-terms."

If you feel any of the symptoms listed on the previous page for the first time, it's important to tell your parents, doctor, or another trusted adult. Like Carlos, you may have no physical problem, but it's important to check it out. For example, some medications cause symptoms that seem like stress. If there is no medical cause for your symptoms, your body may be responding to stress. (See Chapter 2 for some strategies to calm your body's stress response.)

Pay Attention to How You Are Acting

When you are feeling upset or nervous, these emotions can sometimes come out in confusing ways. Have you ever shown your emotions in these ways?

- crying a lot
- getting angry more than usual
- fighting more with friends or family
- being more impulsive
- not trying your best, even if you love what you are doing
- having trouble concentrating
- wanting to give up on the work
- wanting to be alone more

Even when you are not particularly stressed, you may find that your emotions can sometimes change from day to day. This may be because you are changing from a kid to a teenager. You may have new expectations for yourself, such as trying to do well in school in order to get into college. Becoming a preteen can also lead to changes in how you feel about other kids. Your hormones begin to change, too. All of this can cause you to be more emotional than you may have been before, or cause you to swing from one emotion to another.

Sometimes our feelings get so complicated and powerful that we need to talk to someone. Even adults will sometimes call a friend, speak to a husband or wife, or even see a therapist. Think about whom you might talk to if your negative thoughts or emotions overwhelm you. Mae said, "Once I started thinking about it, I had so many people waiting to help me. I knew my mom, my aunt, and my guidance counselor would be supportive. When I started talking, though, I didn't know how to explain what I was feeling. They helped me talk it out."

External Stress

Sometimes students feel that life would be better if only other people would stop stressing them out. Tasha said, "If my teachers wouldn't be so sadistic and keep giving me tests and homework and my parents would stop fighting and my BFF would stop being jealous whenever I talk to anyone else, life would be stress-free!" Do you agree with Tasha?

The pressures Tasha described are called "external stress." External stresses are generally situations around you (in your academic, social, or family life) that can cause you to feel anxious, overwhelmed, upset, or even angry. For example, you may feel stress if you're taking a challenging class, if your best friend since third grade suddenly starts hanging out with other kids, or if your family is pushing you to get As in every subject. All of these examples are *external* causes of stress—they involve people or situations in your life, rather than your internal thoughts or feelings.

External pressures are outside of your control, but you can change how you deal with the stress they create in you. This chapter will help you to identify the possible sources of your stress, and later chapters will offer ideas for how to deal with them.

Common Causes of External Stress

If you are feeling this kind of stress, it could be due to a lot of different causes. Here are some common sources of external stress for students.

Academic concerns. Schoolwork-related stress may be caused by long assignments, having too many assignments, not understanding the work, or feeling that the assignment is harder for you than for other kids.

Time pressures are another common source of schoolwork-related stress. Time pressures can happen when you have a lot of homework one night or when you have long-term projects to do and run out of time. (See Chapter 5 for some strategies to deal with both of these difficulties.)

Sometimes you may want quiet time to study. If your brother or sister is screaming, your parents are talking loudly, or a neighbor stops by for dinner, you may have trouble focusing on your work. This can create tension for some kids.

Social concerns. Social worries can keep students from having the enthusiasm or energy for their school work. Social concerns may include situations such as friends fighting and wanting you to take sides, a friend fighting with you, being left out of a party, or someone teasing or even bullying you.

Family issues. Family issues can lead to stress as well. For example, you may have an argument with your brother or sister, feel upset when your parents are yelling at each other, or learn that your relative is very sick. Stress at home can affect your concentration at school, drain you of energy to do your schoolwork, or make it difficult to get your homework done.

Financial concerns. What if you feel you need a computer to do your school work and you know that your parents can't afford one? What if you need to buy materials for a project? When you feel that you really need something and can't afford it, this can certainly create stress. Even when it's something you know you don't *really* need, like a cool new video game, you can feel tension when you don't have the money to buy it.

Any situation that you view as stressful. Everyone responds to situations differently. There may be some situations that are uniquely stressful for you, but not for others. You may find that any test creates

KIDS' QUESTIONS ANSWERED!

Jamal's Question: **I love my parents but they get down on me when I get grades like an 86, even though I studied really hard. What should I do?**

It's nice to hear that you love your parents and that they want you to do well in school. The challenge seems to be that they may not always be happy with your grades. You mentioned that they may get upset with your grade, even if you studied. It's important to consider the possibility that you and your parents have a different definition of studying.

When you and your parents have some time to really talk, try figuring out answers to these questions:

- Do they expect a certain grade or a certain amount of effort on your part?
- What do they call "studying hard" and what do you mean by this?
- Do you need help in certain subjects?
- Do you put in a lot of time studying, but need help studying better?

Try talking with your parents when you don't have a test paper to show them. This way, they know that you aren't trying to get away with a grade that they may not like, but you are trying to help them to understand you better.

If your parents just want all your grades to be over 90 (or even 95), no matter if you study hard or not, then this is another topic that needs to be discussed. Perhaps your parents want you to go to a top college and feel that you need these high marks. You may want to see if you and your parents can meet with your guidance counselor to discuss expectations. Your guidance counselor can probably understand your efforts to succeed as well as your parents' desire for you to reach your potential.

anxiety and stress, while your friend may actually enjoy taking tests as a way to show how much she learned. Another friend may find long-term projects put pressure on him, while you may find that they can be fun because you love having the time to be creative. There is no right or wrong way to feel about a situation. What is stressful to one person doesn't have to be stressful to another. If you feel stress, then it's time to find ways to deal with it, not deny that the stress is there.

Understand Your External Stress

Now that you've learned some examples of situations that may be stressful to students, it is time to think about your external stresses. Remember that external stresses involve situations, people, or experiences that occur around you or to you. You may want to write them down on the lines below so that you can come back to them and use the strategies you will learn in the following chapters to deal with them.

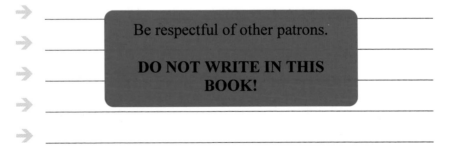

Be respectful of other patrons.

DO NOT WRITE IN THIS BOOK!

Internal Stress

Internal stresses involve your thoughts and feelings. Unlike external stresses, these are stresses that you usually have a lot of control over. They are called "internal stresses" because they happen inside you. For example, the day before you give your oral report in Social Studies, you practice but feel anxious that you might forget what to say. For some people, that anxiety can motivate them to prepare more or find ways to relax. Other people might get overwhelmed by their nerves. So, the same situation can be viewed as exciting, motivating, worrisome, or scary, depending on what you tell yourself and how you think about it. Challenges in life—like giving oral reports, playing sports, or learning how to play a new musical instrument—can be fun as long as the pressures you place on yourself (internal stress) and the pressures others might place on you (external stress) motivate you but don't overwhelm you.

Common Causes of Internal Stress

There are three very common traps that people fall into when it comes to the way they think: perfectionism, negative self-talk, and procrastination. These ways of thinking can all cause internal stress, and not just for students. Many, many adults have these same challenges. Do any of these ways of thinking sound familiar?

Perfectionism. Perfectionism means feeling like you need to be perfect and setting unrealistic standards for yourself. This can put a lot of pressure on kids and keep them from trying new things and having fun. If you try something new for the first time, you probably will not be perfect. Is this okay with you? Or do you get upset if you don't do it correctly and perfectly the first time? If you always need to be the best, the fastest, the smartest, or the most talented, then you may have perfectionistic expectations.

Lots of kids face this difficulty. Miriam explained, "I always wanted the A on my test or a score of 100. I got a score of 91 on my math test and was really annoyed that I missed getting the extra 9 points. Wanting to be perfect was one of my flaws—wanting to be perfect made me not perfect. Think about how weird that is!"

Stuart wanted to have perfect essays and ended up writing, rewriting, crossing out, changing, deleting, and getting frustrated with his assignments, even when his first edits were enough to complete the assignments well. The external pressure of completing the assignments wasn't Stuart's concern; it was his perfectionistic expectations of himself. He wanted to hand in perfect papers, but he ended up not even finishing them on time because of his fears that they would not be perfect.

If you find that you are not motivated to do your best, but only to get a perfect grade, then you may have perfectionistic tendencies. Chapter 2 will discuss some ways to deal with the tension this can create.

Self-doubts or negative self-talk. Did you know that the way you think can add to your stress? Self-doubts are when you beat yourself up with words. This is also called "negative self-talk." If you psych yourself into believing you can't do something well, it's really difficult to focus and try hard.

Have you ever said or thought any of the following?

- "I know I'm going to fail this test."
- "I'm going to forget everything when I get up to give my oral report."
- "I'm just too stupid to learn this stuff."
- "I'll make a fool out of myself if I try."
- "I always do poorly on essay tests."

These kinds of thoughts can make you feel more stressed. This can make it hard to motivate yourself to study, concentrate on tests, do your homework, and finish long-term projects.

Other negative thoughts about your life or situation can also create stress. Here are some examples:

- "My teacher is super hard and hates me."
- "There's not enough time to finish my work."
- "I'll *never* get any peace and quiet to study now that my sister's home from college."
- "I won't make the team; I never have enough time to practice."
- "My brother is always better than me at math anyway."

There are ways to change negative self-talk into positive self-talk. You'll read more about this in Chapter 2.

Procrastination. Procrastination is when you put off doing your work until later or right before the due date. This can occur for many reasons, such as:

- deciding to do more fun things first
- not wanting to deal with the anxiety that the work makes you feel
- pretending you don't have the assignment because it seems hard
- problems with time management
- not being motivated

Sometimes adults assume that you might put off work because you don't care about it. Honestly, this may be true sometimes. It's not always true, though. Say you have a choice of getting a shot at the doctor's office either today or next week. Some kids would want to get it over with, but many kids would choose next week in order to put off the stress of thinking about it.

Procrastination doesn't automatically mean that you are lazy. It can mean that you need to learn better ways to start and follow through on work (see Chapter 5), or it can mean that you need support dealing with the internal stress that the work might create in you (see Chapter 2).

Understand Your Internal Stress

Now that you have learned about some examples, think about your internal stresses. You may want to write them on the lines below, so that you can come back to them and use the strategies you will learn in the following chapters to deal with them.

❋ _____

❋ _____

❋ _____

Can Stress Ever Be Positive?

Do you think that athletes get stressed before they compete in the Olympic games? Do you think that the president of the United States ever feels stress? If so, then why would they put themselves in these positions?

People often think that stress is a bad thing, but it doesn't have to be bad at all. Sometimes stress helps people focus and gives them an "adrenaline rush" of energy to compete in a sport, write a good speech, or concentrate on their school work. It's a matter of how much stress you feel, not whether or not you feel stress.

Beckie is now in eighth grade, but she remembers, "When I was in sixth grade, my friends always said they wished they were calm like me. I never felt stress about anything. I just thought I'd deal with things when they happened. The problem, which became a big problem, was that I never got motivated to study for tests or do long-term projects before the last minute." Beckie used to have low stress and found that it caused low motivation for her to do her work.

Unlike Beckie, Gabe always remembers having stress in his school life. He explained, "I used to start worrying the first day of school when my teacher told us how she would grade us. When I got a project to do, I used to think about it every night. I was too nervous, though, to start it. I just spent my time thinking and being scared that I wouldn't do it right."

So, Beckie and Gabe had opposite levels of stress (low and high, respectively). Neither Beckie nor Gabe seemed to find that the stress worked for them. William, on the other hand, rated his stress level as "in between" or as a 4, 5, or 6 on a scale of 1–10 where 1 is low stress and 10 is high stress. He said, "When I have something to do, I get this feeling of wanting to do it well, but I know that if I need help I can get it.

Stress isn't always a bad thing!

I get more energy to do the work when I'm a little stressed, but I don't worry about how I do it because I have confidence it will work out."

William's stress can be labeled as "positive stress" because it motivates him to take on his responsibilities. A fancy name for positive stress is "eustress."

How do you know if the stress you are experiencing is positive stress? The difference is whether it motivates you or overwhelms you. Notice that Gabe felt so anxious that he didn't start his project. However, William's stress gave him the boost of energy he needed to do his work. Positive stress motivates you to meet a challenge.

You may also experience positive stress when you move outside of your comfort zone to try something new. For example, say you are trying a new sport in gym class. Positive stress can help to motivate you to learn the rules and figure out what to do. Some students even say that positive stress feels just like excitement or a challenge that they want to face.

Now, don't you wish all your stress could be positive stress? Read on to learn some ways to manage your stress so you can make it work for you.

Summary

Congratulations! By reading this first chapter, you began the journey toward understanding stress. You learned the signs and symptoms of stress, both physical and emotional. You learned the difference between internal and external stress, and read about some common causes of stress. You might have even been able to figure out what is causing you stress! In the next chapters, you will read about ways to deal with stress so that you can hopefully be more comfortable at school.

2.

Anxiety-Busting Mind Games

This chapter will help you to find strategies for dealing with internal stress. Do you already use any of the stress-busting strategies in the list below? Check off as many of the boxes that apply.

☐ I know how to turn my negative thoughts into positive ones.

☐ I feel that school is about learning and trying my best, not about being perfect.

☐ When I'm stressed, I remind myself of things I'm good at.

☐ I can visualize myself doing well at my school work.

☐ I have people I can turn to for support when I feel stressed.

☐ I take care of my body by eating well, getting enough sleep, and exercising.

☐ I know relaxation techniques to calm my body when I'm feeling stressed.

If you do use some of these ways to reduce your internal stress, congratulations! This chapter may give you even more ideas. If you don't use any strategies right now, or use some that don't work well, you will learn more techniques in the upcoming pages.

There will be times when you can't change the pressures of school. Imagine if you decided to tell your teacher not to give you a final exam.

It probably wouldn't make your teacher happy, and you would still have to study and take the test. The good news is that there are ways to deal with stress so that you don't feel like you want to scream, throw your pillow against the wall, panic, or cry.

Danger—Negative Mind Games

Negative mind games aren't fun. Negative mind games happen when you try to convince yourself that you can't cope with certain situations, or when you blame other people for your stress rather than seeking a solution. These negative mind games can lead you to feel super stressed and even angry, anxious, or helpless.

You may be playing negative mind games in your head without even realizing it. Eddie was a champ at this. He explained, "I would always tell myself that I'm going to fail or make a fool of myself. I really wanted to do baseball and be in honors science, but I was too scared to even try." Eddie's belief that he would fail or embarrass himself if he tried baseball or honors science kept him from having the experience and the possible pride and fun that comes with new adventures. What about you? Do you ever scare yourself or insult yourself? If you do, you are definitely not alone. Many people avoid situations that might be enjoyable because of their negative mind games.

In Chapter 1, you learned about some common negative mind games, like perfectionism, negative self-talk, and procrastination, and how these negative mind games can cause internal stress. Now, it's time to learn some tools to help you cope with the thoughts and feelings that cause you stress. How you think about the situations that cause you stress can change how you feel about them. If you think, "easier said than done," you may be surprised. Let's get started by putting the coping tools in your tool kit.

Reducing Internal Stress

If you have ever played a videogame, you know that you can imagine yourself in an entirely new galaxy. Obviously, you are still on the planet earth, but you can travel far away in your mind, without much effort. Good news: in school, you can also use these creative skills to feel capable and successful, rather than overwhelmed and upset. It is your choice. Even if you can't change the stress around you, if you consider the possibility that you can change the way you think and feel, then you open the door to dealing with internal stress.

So, how do you play positive mind games to feel more capable and less stressed? Read on to learn some tools that kids have used and found helpful.

Practice Positive Self-Talk

They may not admit it to others, but people talk to themselves a lot! How you talk to yourself—not just what you say out loud, but your inner thoughts as well—can affect how you feel. Kids can use negative self-talk and make life more stressful, or they can change the way they think and talk to support and encourage themselves.

TOOL KIT FOR REDUCING INTERNAL STRESS

- **Practice positive self-talk**
- **Challenge irrational beliefs**
- **Build your confidence**
- **Imagine success**
- **Seek out a support team**

Turn your negative thoughts into positive ones to give yourself support and encouragement.

If you are used to using negative self-talk, it may feel weird to start using positive self-talk. It's like learning a new way to do long division. If you are used to one way of doing something, it may feel right, even though a new way may lead to greater success and, sometimes, even greater happiness.

Here are some examples of ways you can turn negative self-talk into positive self-talk:

- Change "I think I can't," to "I think I can."
- Change "Everyone will laugh at me," to "I may not get everything right at first, and my mistakes may be funny at first. I may laugh too!"
- Change "I have to do it right the first time," to "I'll be happy even if I just show up that first day at tryouts."
- Change "I can't do the project. It's too hard," to "I'll start the project, then ask for help if I need it."
- Change "I'm a loser if I need help," to "Everyone needs help sometimes."

Do the positive thoughts sound more helpful and more realistic? It may take a while to get the hang of it, but if you keep trying, soon it will feel more natural to think positive thoughts. Can you think of any times you have used negative self-talk? Write out three negative thoughts you have had, and replace them with positive ones.

NEGATIVE THOUGHTS:	NEW POSITIVE THOUGHTS:
1.	1.
2.	2.
3.	3.

Challenge Irrational Beliefs

Irrational beliefs are thoughts that you may believe are true, but they really aren't. Lots of kids have irrational beliefs about school. One of the best examples is from Nathan. He said, "I thought that I had to get 100 on my test or else my teacher wouldn't like me and I would feel stupid." Brittany convinced herself that, even in sixth grade, she had to get straight As or she wouldn't get into a good college. Huh? Do you agree with Nathan and Brittany?

School is about learning, not about perfection. No one is perfect at everything and very few are perfect at anything. Even athletes in the Olympics don't always get a gold medal. Even when they get a gold medal, they may not get it the next time they compete. But shouldn't they feel proud of their efforts and accomplishments?

A few tips:

- Remind yourself that trying your best is success.
- Focus on your strengths and remind yourself that you can improve upon your weaknesses.
- Be kind to yourself—other kids may have stronger math skills or may be more outgoing. That doesn't mean there is something wrong with you.
- Pat yourself on the back for your abilities.

See if you can help Adam. Adam was a perfectionist. He knew it, but wasn't sure how to deal with it. Adam used to love basketball because he had the highest overall free-throw percentage of anyone on his team. However, he practiced every night, felt nervous before each game because he felt so much internal stress to make the baskets at the free-throw line, and he felt that he "stunk" on the court if he didn't score higher than the other players. He felt so much pressure that he wasn't even enjoying the game anymore. What could you tell Adam to help him with his perfectionism? Check the responses that might help him:

- [ ] Tell him that it doesn't matter if he's the best free-throw player if he doesn't enjoy himself.

- [ ] Suggest that he might set a realistic goal for free-throw percentages and be okay with missing some, since even the pros do that.

- [ ] Tell him that other kids like to hang out with him even if he misses baskets, so why not like himself even if he misses baskets?

- [ ] When he's being too hard on himself, remind him that he can care about doing his best but he doesn't have to put stress on himself to always be the best.

If you felt that all the answers might help Adam, you are right! However, sometimes it's easier to help someone else than to convince ourselves that we don't have to be perfect. If you are a perfectionist, maybe you can use some of the tips described above for Adam.

Build Your Confidence

When you feel good about yourself, it's easier to take risks, try new experiences, try your best, and apply yourself to studying for tests. If you really believe that you are nice, funny, bright, or caring (or all of these!), then keep reminding yourself of these traits in order to counter negative self-talk. Confidence means that you feel that you can handle external stresses and that you avoid beating yourself up with negative self-talk.

You may wonder if changing the words you say to yourself really matters. It definitely does! It can lessen your internal stress and can even make your work seem less scary, overwhelming, or difficult.

If you keep telling yourself that you can't do things well, you may need some help thinking about what makes you special. It's time to think about your strengths and special qualities—we *all* have them!

If you feel self-confident, it's easier to take risks or try new experiences.

Do you know what strengths or abilities you have? If you have some ideas, write them down in the space below and look at the list whenever you are getting down on yourself. If you don't know of any talents or special qualities that you have, ask your parents, grandparents, friends, or even teachers. Ask anyone who might be able to help you see your positive qualities. Then, add them to your list.

→ _____

→ _____

→ _____

→ _____

→ _____

When you are starting to use negative self-talk, look at your list, remind yourself that you have succeeded before, and try positive self-talk. The more you use positive self-talk the easier it becomes to use it!

Another way to build your confidence is to keep a journal. Vanessa said, "I tried to use the self-talk, but it always felt weird." Vanessa loved to write in her journal, so she wrote about how she could focus on her strengths and how she doesn't have to be perfect. In her journal, she changed her negative thoughts to positive ones. It was more comfortable for Vanessa to write out her thoughts than to just think them in her head. You may find that writing out your thoughts helps you too.

If you like art, you could also try building your confidence through drawing. In your journal, perhaps you can make up a comic strip with the evil negative self-talker challenging the positive self-talker. How can the positive self-talker win? It can be a fun way to try to win over your own self doubts and negative self-talk.

KIDS' QUESTIONS ANSWERED!

Xavier's Question: **How am I supposed to deal with the fact that all of my friends are smarter than me?**

Xavier, many students believe that their friends are smarter, more athletic, more attractive, or funnier than them. Think about why you believe that you are not as smart as your friends. Is it possible that your friends:

- just have better study habits?
- ask more questions in class, so they understand the material better?
- don't give up as quickly as they get frustrated?
- also silently question their intelligence?

Guess what! You can't know everything about everything. Someone else is probably always going to know more about something than you. Just because another student has an area of strong knowledge, this doesn't mean that he or she is smarter than you.

Confidence can help you ask questions, give opinions, and even respond more quickly to situations. Xavier, if you don't feel smart, try building your confidence by thinking about your strengths and using positive self-talk. If you still feel like everyone else is smarter, you might want to talk with your teacher, guidance counselor, or parent. They can point out your strengths and abilities, and help you figure out if there is something that you can work on in order to learn more easily.

Imagine Success

If you always imagine failure, it's hard to plan for success. If you imagine success, then it becomes a possibility.

Of course, fantasy will not lead to instant success. Just because you imagine walking into Spanish class for the first time, hearing your teacher speak to you in this foreign language, and then answering him in fluent Spanish, it doesn't mean you can actually learn Spanish instantly. If your goal is to speak Spanish fluently, imagine succeeding at each small step that you need to do in order to get to be better and better at the vocabulary, accent, and grammar of this new language.

In school, it can be helpful to focus on each step of your work, not everything you need to do for the semester. If you set realistic goals, then imagine succeeding at the first steps, then the next steps, and so on, the goals become more realistic and more manageable. Imagining success at each step can be a great way to remind yourself that you can take on the challenge.

Try to set realistic goals that you can generally reach within a few weeks (or days, even), so that you can have success. You may want to try using the ladder on the next page. For example, Tara wanted to bake. The bottom step for Tara was to learn what each of the measurement symbols meant (such as a teaspoon versus a tablespoon). The next step up on Tara's ladder was for her to make sure that she had all the baking ingredients. If she wanted to be a top baker on her first day in the kitchen, she probably would have felt frustrated and disappointed. So, it's important to pick realistic goals. Take a minute to create your own realistic step-by-step ladder so that you can realistically reach each step and each goal.

Imagining success can help you achieve it!

Your goals!

8.

7.

6.

5.

4.

3.

2.

1.

Seek Out a Support Team

Having a support team is not a sign of weakness. In fact, it's smart to surround yourself with people who can help. Isn't it better to get help before a social studies test so that you can understand the material than to avoid asking for help and not do well? If you look at the adults around you, they probably all get help sometimes. A doctor may want help from an IT expert to set up her computer. A mechanic may be able to fix a lawyer's car, while the lawyer may be able to help the mechanic. Knowing who to go to for help, and seeking them out, is a sign of being resourceful, clever, and motivated.

On the lines below, write down the people in your life who you could trust and turn to for support.

_____

_____

_____

_____

_____

Now, if you aren't used to asking for help, what could you say? Here are some tips:

- Be clear and specific. Rather than saying "I don't get math," try saying, "I don't get the steps to these algebra questions. What do I do first?"

- Let the person know that you want to get help so you can gain the skills to be more independent later. Rather than saying, "I want you to do this for me," you might say, "I tried to do this but I'm confused. Can you help me figure out what I'm supposed to do with these vocabulary words so I can do the homework sheet on my own?"

In the lines below, write what you might say to a member of your support team to get the help you need:

→ _____

→ _____

→ _____

→ _____

→ _____

Taking Care of Yourself Physically

Since you can't separate your brain from your body, it's important to take care of your body. If your body is tired or hungry, you will probably find that you aren't super alert to study. If you've just come home from an amazing party, you probably need time to calm your body before you can focus on your work. Just like an athlete trains for a big game, you can train your body so you perform your best at school. If you take care of your body by having healthy eating habits, sleeping well, and exercising regularly, you can feel your best and be ready to take on the challenges of school and homework.

Taking care of your body by eating healthy food helps to fuel your mind.

Eat Healthy Food
You may have heard this (maybe a million times!) from adults already: You are what you eat. Before you roll your eyes, think about how a car doesn't run without gas. Our bodies rely on food to fuel them to work well. This advice is not about avoiding certain foods or eating the foods that make you want to gag. That's the good news!

The reality, though, is that a healthy diet does affect your body and often affects how your mind works. If you try to eat foods from the different food groups, and eat regularly throughout the day, you will probably find that you focus better and have more energy to work. Even if you have a busy schedule, you can find ways to eat well. Don said, "My dad and I make my sandwiches for the week on Sunday nights. In the mornings, I just grab my sandwich, a piece of fruit, and a small salad from the refrigerator. It takes planning, but it's easy during the week. I make sure I eat, even if I'm busy talking with my friends. If I go for extra help, I ask if I can eat a bag of nuts or dried fruit while I'm talking with the teacher. Eating right isn't hard if you plan ahead." You may want to try Don's strategy.

Get Enough Sleep

You may notice that your sleep schedule changes as you become a teenager. Sometimes kids believe that they actually need very little sleep, when in fact the opposite is true. Sleep is a great study tool. While you are asleep, your brain has a chance to recharge and it gets the rest that it needs. If you often lose sleep because you cram for big tests, keep reading—Chapters 6 and 7 will cover ways to avoid cramming.

If you have trouble falling asleep, see if you can figure out why. If you are up all night texting or on the computer, try to come up with a plan to deal with this. You may want to make a pact with friends to stop texting at a certain time, or find another creative strategy. For example, Leslie said, "I used to be addicted to texting and never got enough sleep. Then I decided to tell my friends that my parents won't let me use my phone after 9:30 at night. My parents actually agreed to being blamed. My friends were fine with this and I got more sleep!"

You may find that it is easier to fall asleep if you stick to a routine. Try to go to bed at the same time each night. A half-hour before you turn off your lights, find an activity that relaxes you and prepare yourself for sleep. Exercising or frantically studying for a test are not great ways to calm yourself and prepare for sleep, and can even keep you awake. Try reading a book, listening to soothing music, or writing in a journal instead.

Exercise Regularly

Exercise is always an important part of keeping your body healthy. You may need to experiment to find a time to exercise that works for you. Sometimes kids are too tired after working out to study. Sometimes kids are too tired to study until they exercise! Just be careful not to exercise right before bed.

Many people find that exercise helps them relax. There are many different ways to get exercise, such as joining a sports team, doing an individual sport such as tennis or swimming, going to a gym and working out, or getting involved in a non-competitive physical activity like yoga, dance, or martial arts. Even walking around the block is good for your health! Before starting any exercise program, though, make sure that your doctor clears you to do it.

Relaxation Techniques

Relaxation techniques are also important tools to have in your tool box. There are many relaxation techniques to pick from. Check out the strategies below to see if any might be a good fit for you.

TOOL KIT FOR RELAXATION

- **Use all five senses**
- **Practice breathing exercises**
- **Try progressive muscle relaxation**
- **Shake and relax**
- **Count backwards**
- **Meditate**

Use All Five Senses

You can create imaginary scenes using all, some, or even just one of your senses to help you relax. Imagine this scene: You are at the beach, watching the waves slowly wash onto shore, then slowly go back into the ocean. You hear the gentle crashing of the waves and the song of a seagull in the distance. You feel the slight breeze against your cheek, feel the sand beneath your toes, and you smell and taste the salt air from the water.

This imaginary scene uses all five senses—sight, sound, touch, smell, taste. Some kids really can imagine this and it takes them to a calmer place. What about you?

Here are some more examples of imaginary scenes, using your senses, that have helped other kids and may help you too:

- being hugged by a favorite grandparent and smelling their perfume or after-shave
- hugging your favorite pet
- laying in a hammock in the backyard on a beautiful day

There are really no limits. You are free to imagine whatever helps you to relax. Also, once you get good at imagining it, you can quickly conjure up your favorite relaxing scene. What a great tool!

If you are lucky enough, you can use real situations for stress relief. For example:

- Jeff used to go for long walks with his dad.
- Roberta loved to sit at the park with her dog and watch the trees sway with the wind.
- Hailey liked to lie in bed listening to music and petting her cat for a little while after school. This helped her to feel more relaxed and ready to study.

> Relaxation techniques help calm your mind, feelings, and body.

Practice Breathing Exercises

Clearly, you know how to breathe. You do it all the time! So, why are you reading about how to do it? Actually, there are changes to your breathing that may happen when you are stressed. Some kids find they accidentally hold their breath. Other kids breathe shallow breaths from the top of their chest rather than from their diaphragm (near their stomach). As you learned in Chapter 1, changes in your breathing can help you run from wild animals but not from a test.

There are ways to use your breathing to help you calm down. Here's how:

1. Take a deep breath (through your nose, if you can).
2. Try to focus all your thoughts on your breathing.
3. Hold your breath for three seconds.
4. Slowly let the air out through your mouth.
5. Do steps one through four all over again, three times.

Do you feel calmer? If so, then this is a good strategy for you. If you find that you feel too relaxed to focus, then you may want to try a different strategy. Check with your doctor if you feel lightheaded or dizzy.

Try Progressive Muscle Relaxation

You can actually use the tension or stress in your body to help you relax. If you try this tool, just remember to breathe. Sometimes kids find that they hold their breath during this exercise, and it's certainly less fun without oxygen!

Progressive muscle relaxation is a three-step technique:

1. Scrunch, crunch, or tense up your muscles. Start with your forehead. If you are doing this correctly, you may feel like you are making wrinkles.

KIDS' QUESTIONS ANSWERED!

Claire's Question: **Sometimes I feel like I can't breathe before a test. Can you help me?**

Claire, if you only have breathing problems before tests, it is probably due to your stress, but mention it to your doctor anyway.

It's important to figure out whether you are having internal stress before tests. Internal stress can be caused by what you say to yourself. An example would be if you tell yourself that, "Even though I studied, I'm going to fail. I just know I will!" You can work to change your internal thinking. Try to think more positive thoughts instead, such as, "I studied hard. If I get questions wrong, I can just get help to understand them later."

If you feel nervous because of external stress, remember that there are also ways to cope with this. Let's say that you have a math test on Thursday, but you are up late on Wednesday nights at gymnastics. Can you ask your coach if you could leave early that night or switch your practice night? Could you study before going to gymnastics?

If you start to feel that you can't breathe, these relaxation exercises might help:

- Try using your five senses to think of relaxing scenes.
- Use breathing exercises—take slow, deep breaths, then slowly exhale.
- Try progressive muscle relaxation.
- You can also try the shake and relax activity, counting backwards, and meditation.

See which one of these helps you to catch your breath before a test.

2 Hold the muscle crunch for three seconds.

3 Then, try to totally relax that body part as you exhale deeply.

Start scrunching each body part from the very top of your head down to the tips of your toes. Focus on one small area of your body at a time: first your forehead, then your eyes, then your nose, then your cheeks, then your chin, then your neck, and so forth. Once you are done, you will have tensed and relaxed each part of your body.

The muscle crunches should never hurt. Also, since this involves your body, just check with your doctor to get the okay to do this.

Shake and Relax

Have you ever shaken off a writer's cramp in your wrist? If so, you probably already know how to "shake and relax." It simply involves gently moving or shaking a body part and then focusing on that area being relaxed. The key trick here is to gently move your muscles, not to see how fast or how hard you can accomplish shaking your body.

This tool is used to deal with muscle cramps, but can be great for stress and tension as well. So, shake it off!

Count Backwards

This tool is not about working on your math skills. The idea is to make your brain focus on counting backwards in order to take your concentration away from your stressful thoughts. For example, you can try counting backward slowly from 20 to 1. Or, you may want to count backward from 30 by threes. Once you begin, hopefully, you will find that counting gives you a break from your internal stress. If you like numbers, try counting backward by sevens, starting at 100. It's not a race, so take your time.

You may find that counting adds stress. If so, then this is the wrong technique for you!

Meditate

Once you become skilled at using the tools described in this chapter, you may want to start combining them. This combination does not have to take a lot of time. For instance, you can take deep breaths while visualizing yourself in a comforting place. Sometimes, this combined plan is referred to as meditation.

Meditation can include many different relaxing strategies, such as repeating a word over and over (e.g., "calm"), clearing your mind, and just focusing on the sound of your breathing. Think about a combination that you like and then try it out!

Summary

In this chapter, you read about ways to fight off internal stress. You learned about positive self-talk, focusing on your abilities, imagining success, building confidence, and you learned many different relaxation techniques. The importance of having a healthy body, asking for help when you need it, and avoiding negative self-talk was also reviewed. Now that you know how to manage internal stress, the next chapter will cover some tools to manage external stress.

3.

Coping With External Stresses: An Advanced Tool Set

This chapter focuses on external stresses—situations around you that cause you to feel anxious, overwhelmed, upset, or even angry. It will show you how to figure out what is causing you stress, and ways to handle these stresses. Before you begin this chapter, take a moment to check off which, if any, of the sentences below apply to you:

☐ I know how to figure out what is causing me stress.

☐ I focus my efforts on the part of the situation that is under my control.

☐ I can brainstorm different ways to deal with the stressful situation.

☐ I know how to start making things better for myself.

☐ I can tell if my plan to make things better is working.

There will be times when stress is not coming from your thoughts or feelings but from school and other life pressures. You may believe that you can't change these pressures. Unfortunately, sometimes you are right. For example, you may want your uncle to get married on a different weekend, since you need to study for mid-terms. It's unlikely that your uncle will change the date of the wedding. Luckily, there are strategies to cope with your stress about the situation.

There are times when kids feel stressed, but they aren't even sure what is causing it. Anna, for instance, experienced many stresses before she even got to school. See how many of her stresses you can pick out.

Anna explained, "I usually don't wake up by my alarm, but I was really tired because my brothers were fighting last night and I couldn't fall asleep. I ended up jumping out of bed when the alarm on my cell phone started blasting. It was so loud. Once I got out of bed, I started rushing to get dressed. I had a quiz in my first period French class and couldn't be late. Just before running out to catch the bus, I sat down to eat a quick breakfast and watch the TV in the kitchen. There was a newscaster that interrupted my show with lots of news about how people are going crazy and countries are having riots. On the bus to school, I tried to review my notes for the test but my friend Michaela told me that she's moving and I couldn't think of anything else. I was exhausted by the time I got to school."

Let's review the different stresses that Anna faced before she even got to school:

- being tired because of getting to sleep late
- dealing with the fact that her brothers were fighting the night before
- being shocked out of a deep sleep by a loud, annoying alarm
- needing to rush to get ready
- getting ready for a quiz first period
- learning of some upsetting news from the morning news show
- not having time to review her notes on the bus
- learning that her friend is moving
- feeling exhausted from lack of sleep *and* so much stress

Did you pick out all of these stresses? No wonder Anna is feeling exhausted. If she had a time machine and could rewind the events, how many could she change? Anna couldn't change the fact that her brothers fought. She could have used music or other distractions to fall asleep, though. She might have had a softer alarm clock to wake her. She couldn't change the fact that she had a quiz first period or that there was violence in the world. However, she can decide whether she wants to learn of the news before taking a test or if she would rather wait until later. That's a personal choice. She had no power to keep her friend, Michaela, from moving, but she may have wanted to review her French notes before getting on the bus so she didn't need that extra study time.

If you feel external stress because of things you don't have control over, it's not time to give up. You have control of your thoughts and feelings about the situation. This chapter will show you some ways to deal with these external stresses.

Dealing With External Stress

It's difficult when the cause of your stress is outside of your control. The good news is that there are problem-solving and reframing strategies that can lead to a more positive mindset and reduce your stress. They're a little tricky at first, but with practice, they will become easier. If you follow the step-by-step instructions below, you may have an easier time managing stressful situations that are outside of your control.

TOOL KIT FOR BUSTING EXTERNAL STRESS

- Be a detective
- Focus on what you can change
- Brainstorm options to change your path
- Pick your path and make a plan
- Decide how to implement your plan
- Review if you succeeded

Step 1: Be a Detective

Before you can figure out how to deal with stress, you need to act like a detective and figure out what is causing you stress, as you did with Anna's situation. It may seem obvious that if you feel stress, you know why. However, many kids and adults sometimes struggle to find the cause of their stress when they are just trying to get through their day.

Have you ever felt really upset about your school assignments and tests and felt like crying or yelling? This feeling may not be just about your assignments and tests. If you usually deal with the stress of homework and tests well, but suddenly feel overwhelmed, there may be something else going on. For example, perhaps your confidence is lower because you didn't make it to the finals in the geography bee, you missed an easy question on a test yesterday, or you didn't make it onto the varsity lacrosse team. Maybe your best friend was out sick and she usually gives you a pep talk when you are stressed.

If you figure out that the tests and homework really are what's causing your stress, then you can work on strategies for dealing with your schoolwork. If, however, your schoolwork is not the underlying or real cause, then it's time to deal with what really made you more sensitive, emotional, or stressed (e.g., disappointment about how you did at the geography bee).

For example, let's see how Anna figured out what was causing her stress. First, she spoke with the school guidance counselor about her stressful morning. She was able to figure out all of the stresses that were described earlier in this chapter. After talking about it, though, she realized that there were only two major things that were different from other days:

- learning of the rioting that occurred overnight in other countries, which led to her no longer feeling safe in the world
- learning that Michaela will be moving

> **Once you figure out what is causing you stress, you can begin dealing with it.**

Before going on to Step 2, it's important for you to be your own detective. Anna learned that she really had two external stresses that led to her feeling like she was going to melt down on that stressful morning. Have you ever had a stressful day, like Anna? Take a minute to think like a detective. What was really causing you to feel overwhelmed? Remember, this chapter is focused on the stresses around you and not just about your internal thoughts. Write down your list of "causes"—the underlying sources of your stress—in the space below:

→ _____ _____

→ _____

→ _____ _____

→ _____ _____

→ _____ _____ _____

Step 2: Focus on What You Can Change

Now that you know what is causing your stress, it's time to focus on what you want to have happen and how you can make a change. Here are a few questions to ask yourself:

Is the change you want realistic? Think about what you can and cannot change. For instance, you may wish that your parent would stop working late, but you realize that you can't force this to happen. However, you can talk to your parent about how you feel, because your action is what you can control. For another example, what if you wish that you could give a class presentation to the teacher without the other kids in the room, but the teacher says that the other kids need to be there? You could voice your concern and ask the teacher for suggestions.

As you try to find your own goal, make sure that you have the ability to reach it. When Anna tried to focus on her goals, she first thought, "I want everyone in the world to be friends and I don't want my friend to move." Later, she realized that she can't force everyone to get along, and her friend's family needed to move even if she didn't want this to happen. Anna decided on more realistic goals:

- learn conflict resolution skills, so that she could use them and teach them to others
- find ways to stay close with her friend Michaela, even after Michaela moves away

Both of these goals are under Anna's control.

Can you change how you view the situation? Sometimes you can't change a stressful situation, just like Anna can't change the fact that her friend is moving. Sometimes you don't want to change the situation, even if it's stressful. For example, you may be excited to be in an accelerated or honors class, even though you now have more work.

If you can't or don't want to actually change the situation, but you want to feel less stress about it, many of the strategies you read about in Chapter 2 could help you here. In addition, there is a cool technique called "reframing" that you could try.

Have you ever been to an art museum and seen the really fancy frames for the paintings? Even if the painting is really nice, the frame can make it look even better or, possibly, worse. Sometimes a museum will reframe a painting to make the colors, features, or theme stand out.

When you reframe your view of a situation, you are changing what theme you focus on and what thoughts you highlight. Anna did this with great success. For instance, instead of wanting everyone in the entire world to stop fighting with each other, she reframed this perception and said, "I know that most people don't fight. The

KIDS' QUESTIONS ANSWERED!

Danny's Question: **What do I do when my teacher hates me when I'm just answering her questions in class?**

Danny, the first thing you need to do is think like a detective. What about your teacher's behavior leads you to believe she "hates" you? Here are some questions you could think about:

- Does your teacher ever say "nice job" or compliment you for your answers? If so, when?
- Does she prefer kids to give short answers or long, detailed answers when they talk in class?
- How does she react when she talks with you one-on-one?
- Does she treat you differently than the other kids? If so, how?
- Is she more or less upset when you answer seriously than when you joke?

Once you have these answers, you can begin to figure out whether your teacher's style is just uncomfortable for you (if she treats everyone the same way) or if she really is reacting differently to you. Also, the answers to the questions above may help you to narrow down what expectations your teacher might have for your behavior in the classroom. Once you have this information, you could decide whether you should rethink how often, or how, you answer questions.

If there is nothing you can do to change how your teacher reacts to you, try to reframe your view of the situation. Here are some things you can do:

- Tell yourself that you are a great kid and your other teachers like you (your friends and family do, too!).
- Remind yourself that this is only one class and it will be over at the end of the semester.

If you feel that you are truly being mistreated or misjudged, think about people you can turn to for help.

> **Even when you can't change a situation, you can change how you feel about it!**

newscaster just doesn't cover that. I want to learn conflict resolution skills to make my world a little better." Anna was no longer focused on the riots. She was focused on the fact that most communities do not have riots. This reframing helped her to feel less stress and let her focus more on her French quiz.

Now, think about your goal and how you can focus on the positive and make the goal manageable.

Can you reach your goal in the next few days, week, or month (rather than the next year or years)? There are times when kids pick some wonderful goals, but it would take a year, or even many years, to reach them. If you want to be a lawyer, but you are only 12 now, you can keep that long-term goal, but focus on what you need to do today, tomorrow, or next month to reach current goals. For example, getting organized for studying can help you today and also is a valuable skill if you do end up becoming a lawyer.

If you reach your goal, will you really be happier? Many kids dream of being accepted by the super cool group at school. Becoming a part of this group, though, may mean losing some of their old, close friends and experiencing a great deal of peer pressure to continue to be allowed in the group. So, reaching the goal and joining the super cool group may not make these kids any happier.

In school, if you try to do the best social studies research project ever (that is, if you try to be "perfect"), and spend every night for weeks working on it, *and* you get a good grade, are you happier? If you gave up going to your cousin's birthday party, trying out for your favorite sports team at school, and you missed out on the season finale of the television show you always watch, was it worth it?

You may feel it was worth working constantly for this brief period of time. But you may feel that you need to change your goal from always studying to studying *and* finding time to do other things.

(If this is one of your goals, Chapter 6 will help you develop time management skills.)

If you have competing goals, can you select one? Let's say that you want to do well on a project for school but also want to socialize and get involved in sports or other activities. If you do not have enough time to do everything, can you pick the top goal or goals for the next day or week? This is important to think about before moving to the next step.

Anna's top goal for that morning was to prepare for her French test. She also wanted to hang out with her friend Michaela every minute of every day to feel better about her moving. Anna decided to tell Michaela that she needed to put her feelings of disappointment and sadness about the move on hold and focus on the test until 11:15 a.m. that morning. The two girls agreed to talk about other things until Anna's test was over. They met at 11:25 a.m. for lunch, when they could focus on how they could hold onto their friendship, even though they will be separated.

Think back to the external stresses you listed in Step 1. Is there anything you can change about the situation? Can you change how you view the situation? Think of what you want to change, and write your goal here. Remember to make your goal realistic, something you can achieve in the next few days, weeks, or months, and consider if it will actually make you happier.

_____

_____

_____

_____

_____

Step 3: Brainstorm Options to Change Your Path

Think about how you want to reach your goal and the positive, or possibly negative, results of this choice. One way to do this is to write your goal at the top of a piece of paper. Then list one way to reach your goal. Under that, put the pros (good results) and cons (bad results) of that path. Then, move on to another path. Once you are finished brainstorming possible ways to reach your goal, see which path has the most positive and least negative consequences.

Keith, who played on the junior varsity tennis team, wanted to be accepted by the older kids on the varsity tennis team. He thought about trying to run into them at lunch. On his brainstorming page, he wrote one positive outcome—he thought that lunch time was probably a good time to talk with them. He wrote several negative outcomes, including that his lunch period was at a different time so he would need to cut class in order to hang out with them. After looking over his whole brainstorming list, he ruled out cutting class because of the real serious negative consequences. He decided to cheer on the team after school when they were competing against other schools. He also decided to see if any of the kids could give him tips to make his tennis playing better. Both of these ideas had a lot of positive consequences for Keith.

Anna had to think of her options to teach conflict resolution skills and to keep in touch with her friend. You, like Anna, can write down your goal and the different paths you might take to reach it. Remember to think about the good and bad outcomes for each possible choice. Check out Anna's brainstorming sheet to see how she thought through her options:

Brainstorm different paths to reach your goal, and consider the pros and cons of each path.

Goal: Keep in touch with Michaela

Plan #1: Skype during every lunch period at school so my other friends can join in

Pro:
- a lot of time with Michaela
- it's like she's at lunch with me
- she keeps in touch with other kids too

Con:
- she may have a different lunch time at her new school
- we aren't supposed to be Skyping at my school

Plan #2: Every night, we'll Skype or talk on the phone

Pro:
- a lot of time with Michaela

Con:
- we may not have time for our homework
- we may not be free at the same time
- we may feel like we need to give up other plans just to be home at that time each night to talk

Plan #3: Weekly phone call

Pro:
- we can still keep really close with each other
- we can catch up on the news of each other's lives
- we don't have to give up other plans to be home every night to talk

Con:
- sometimes we may miss a phone call

Step 4: Pick Your Path and Make a Plan

This is actually a quick step. Once you find the best path from your brainstorming list, you have finished this step! Congratulations. You now know how you will move forward!

Goal: Keep in touch with Michaela

Plan #1: Skype during every lunch period at school so my other friends can join in

Pro:
- a lot of time with Michaela
- it's like she's at lunch with me
- she keeps in touch with other kids too

Con:
- she may have a different lunch time at her new school
- we aren't supposed to be Skyping at my school

Plan #2: Every night, we'll Skype or talk on the phone

Pro:
- a lot of time with Michaela

Con:
- we may not have time for our homework
- we may not be free at the same time
- we may feel like we need to give up other plans just to be home at that time each night to talk.

Plan #3: Weekly phone call

Pro:
- we can still keep really close with each other
- we can catch up on the news of each other's lives
- we don't have to give up other plans to be home every night to talk

Con:
- sometimes we may miss a phone call

Step 5: Decide How to Implement Your Plan

Now that you have a plan, take some deep breaths, then decide when and how to start. Anna, for example, realized that she really can't teach conflict resolution skills right now. Her short-term goal was to learn more about it, so she signed up for a conflict-resolution class. She explained, "Later, once I really learn the skills, I'll brainstorm ways to teach others about it." For Anna's second goal of staying close with Michaela, the two girls brainstormed together and decided to keep in touch with a weekly phone call.

You have read a lot about picking your goal. Now, take a few minutes to figure out how you will actually start to reach your goal. It is often helpful to check with your parents, a teacher, or your friends to see if they have any other suggestions or concerns about your choice of action.

Step 6: Review If You Succeeded

Once you begin working towards your goal, stop and check if everything is going well. If it is going smoothly, keep at it! If there are problems, figure out if you need to pick another choice from your brainstorming sheet in order to reach your goal.

Anna actually hit two snags. First, she finished her training in conflict resolution but had no idea how to use it in school. She checked with her guidance counselor and, together, they started a conflict resolution club that became very popular. Second, Anna and Michaela sometimes couldn't stick to their weekly phone time because of family or school responsibilities. They decided that if one of them missed the call, they would just send a quick e-mail or text and try to reschedule for that week. With these two additions to Anna's plan, she felt that she was successful in reaching both of her goals.

If you also hit snags, be creative and try to find ways to adjust your plan so you still reach your goals.

Examples of Kids' Goals and Plans

You've read about how Anna used problem-solving to deal with her external stresses. Here are some more examples of kids' goals, and the plans that they've brainstormed to reach their goals.

School Concerns

Zena's Goal: Learn how to overcome her frustration when she finds that her teacher is not interesting.

Zena's Plan: Participate more in class, because that helps her to feel involved and interested. Reframe the situation to emphasize that not every teacher is super exciting, but this teacher isn't mean at all and will teach her some important topics.

Social Concerns

Evie's Goal: Stop getting stuck in the middle when her friends fight.

Evie's Plan: Talk to each of her friends, privately, about how she cares about them but hates being put in the middle. If they fight again, say, "Please, please, don't put me in the middle." Tell her friends that the guidance counselor can help with friends having problems and they might want to seek him out.

World Concerns

Matthew's Goal: Help reduce hunger in the world.

Matthew's Plan: Get approval from the principal to start a food drive for a local food pantry. Get permission to write a paper for English class on the seriousness of this topic and share it with the class. Ask his dad if they can volunteer at a food pantry.

Family Concerns

Brian's Goal: Find time for studying and dealing with feelings about his grandmother moving in with his familiy after being diagnosed with a serious illness.

Brian's Plan: Be creative about finding a place and time to study. Talk with his older sister about his worries so he can then concentrate on his homework. Make a "caring" card weekly, and give a daily hug and smile to his grandmother.

Your Turn!

Remember the goal you wrote down in Step 2? You may want to try using the other steps in this chapter to problem-solve some ways to reach your goal. Remember to think about the pros and cons of each path to reach your goal. When you've decided on the best plan, you can write it down in the space below.

My Goal:

➡ _____

➡ _____

My Plan:

➡ _____

➡ _____

Summary

In this chapter, you learned the steps to figure out what might be causing you stress, whether you can change the situation or just your thoughts, and ways to problem-solve. Feeling less stressed yet? The next chapter will cover some specific ways to organize your schoolwork and keep track of your assignments to help you deal with the stresses of managing your work.

4.

Organization and Preparation

Organization and preparation are essential if you want to study or work on a project. At home, you need a strategy for organizing your papers and setting up your homework environment so that you can get started on assignments and prepare for tests. Take a minute to check off any of these things that you already do:

☐ I have a system for organizing my school papers and computer files.

☐ I remember to bring home all the books and notebooks that I need so I will be able to do my homework.

☐ If I am confused by an assignment, I ask my teachers for help before leaving school.

☐ I know the best time to study, so I am alert and focused.

☐ I know where I study best (e.g., my bedroom, the kitchen, or the school library).

☐ I know how long I can study without getting distracted or too tired.

☐ I take books out of my backpack as I need them, then put them back so they're ready for the next day.

☐ I make sure I have all the materials I will need within easy reach.

Did you check off any? If you did, congratulations! You have some good strategies for keeping on top of things at school and home. If you left some (or all) of the boxes blank, don't worry! Successful people don't know everything, but they are willing to learn and use what they learn.

This chapter will focus on *organization* and *preparation*. Organization and preparation are two executive functions—skills that help you focus and get stuff done. The next chapter will cover more executive functions to help you study, but for now, let's get started on pre-study organization and preparation.

Step 1: Organization

Remember the calming strategies that you learned in the earlier chapters? First, take a few minutes to calm your mind so that you can focus on the information in this chapter. When you are relaxed, it is easier to focus on being prepared and organized. Once you are prepared and organized to begin your work, you feel better able to take on your assignments so that you can perform your best in school.

Are you relaxed? Great! Now, let's focus on getting organized.

TOOL KIT FOR GETTING ORGANIZED
- **Keep notes and papers in their proper place**
- **Organize your computer files**
- **Remember to bring home the right materials**
- **Understand the homework assignments before leaving school**

Keep Notes and Papers in Their Proper Place

This topic may not sound super fun or interesting. But the truth is, organizational strategies can help you feel less stressed when it's time to study. Really! You know where your papers are so you don't have to look for them. You can also start studying right away, and finish earlier, if you don't have to spend time looking for the materials that you need. So, try to hang in there and read about organizational strategies.

Starting on the first day of school, you probably receive a lot of papers—course outlines, class rules, test and quiz schedules—not to mention all the homework, class notes, and quiz papers you will accumulate over the school year. It makes sense to put all those papers in a folder for that class, right? But what happens when you have a lot of papers from your social studies teacher, math teacher, English teacher, science teacher, and foreign language teacher? Do you always put the papers or old tests in the separate folders or binders? Or does everything end up in one big stack in your backpack or locker?

Marcus admitted, "I had a filing system. I put everything into my backpack. I thought that I would figure out what to do with the papers later. I was always too busy leaving class to bother getting really organized. What happened was that I didn't know what I had. Papers got crumbled at the bottom of my bag, with some old food, and I was totally a mess with organization."

Sound familiar? There are lots of different filing systems that work for kids. Here are a couple of systems that could work for you if you don't have an organization plan in place already. Pick one that you think might work best for you and try it out. Just check that it's okay with all of your teachers.

> Organizing your work takes a few minutes every day. Fixing disorganization takes much longer.

Keep a different notebook and folder for each subject. With this option, you have one folder and one notebook for each of your subjects. So, for instance, your science folder and one of your notebooks would only have science material in them. You would have another folder and notebook for social studies, and another notebook and folder for math, and so forth. So when you are in math class, you only have to get out one notebook and folder. At the end of class, you can put whatever papers or assignments you get in your math folder. This way, you organize your stuff for each subject separately, so papers from other classes don't get mixed up with your math class papers.

If you like this strategy, it might be helpful to color-code your materials differently for each subject. Because folders and notebooks often come in a variety of colors, this can be an effective and easy method to get organized. Let's say you decide that green will be the color for science. Get a green folder for all your science papers, homework, and assignments. Get a green notebook to use as your "science notebook." Or, if you don't have green folders and notebooks, you can draw a symbol in green marker on the folder tab and the front of the notebook. So when you are looking for your science materials, you just need to look for the green-marked folder and notebook. Once you find the green color, you know that you have what you need for science class. Jackie found, "This system worked for me. I color-coded the top and bottom of the notebooks too and it was so easy to just grab the right notebook and folder. I wish I had this system last year!" Jackie also had one multi-colored folder for papers from all subjects that were supposed to be left at home.

If you use this strategy, you may end up having five folders and five notebooks. This might not work for all kids. So think about it—are you the kind of person who might feel rushed and grab the closest folder when you have to put away papers? Do you tell yourself that you'll put the paper in the right notebook at night, but never seem to have time for that? If this describes you, then having lots of folders and notebooks

KIDS' QUESTIONS ANSWERED!

Priya's Question: **Why is it so easy for everyone else to keep their locker and their backpack organized? I can't seem to figure it out.**

Priya, being organized is a skill. Just like some kids are better at social studies than at science, some kids are better at organization than other kids. Luckily, you can get better with practice.

Here are a few ways to get organized:

- Find a filing system for putting your loose papers away and taking notes that works for you.

- Use one homework pad for all subjects to remember what needs to be done at night.

- Use a checklist or check off items from your homework pad to help you pack up the right books to bring home.

- Try spending a few minutes once a week cleaning out your locker and going through your backpack to get re-organized. Throw out old food and put papers that you don't need now, but may need later, in a "Stay at Home" folder and bring it home.

may give you too many choices for where to put your papers. Samantha loved this strategy during the first week of school, but then found, "I got frustrated. Too many folders and notebooks to sort through to find the right one for each class."

PAPER ORGANIZATION STRATEGY #2:

Use an accordion folder and a five-section notebook to keep all your work in one place. Accordion folders generally have sections and open wider when more papers are in them. You could use an accordion folder for *all* your papers. Because accordion folders have different sections, you just need to label one section for each subject. So, for example, you would have a section labeled "MATH" for your math papers. You don't need to find which folder to use. There's only *one* to grab from your backpack!

When it comes to your notebooks, you can see if your teachers would allow you to use a five-section notebook. Five-section notebooks have tabs where you can write the subject name, so you can go right to that section for writing notes. You only have one notebook for all your subjects, so it's easy to find in your backpack.

This system is great for some students. Laura said, "With this plan, I always had everything with me. I just made sure I got my notebook and accordion folder before going home." However, William didn't like this plan. He explained, "I hated dragging everything around with me. Why bring my Spanish notes home if I don't have any Spanish homework? My backpack already weighs a ton."

PAPER ORGANIZATION STRATEGY #3:

Sort your notes and papers when you get home. Strategy #3 takes extra time, so it may not work for most kids, but it may be the best for you. If you feel like you don't have time at school to use strategy #1 or #2 and just want to throw everything into your backpack, then think about using this plan.

With this strategy, you have a notebook with just blank pages and an empty file folder. Each morning, you can bring your organized subject notebooks and folders to class in case you need them, but you only write your notes in the blank notebook and put handouts in the one empty file folder. You don't worry about where they go until later. Once you get home, you take your notebook out, carefully remove the papers and put them into the appropriate notebook for the subject.

If you are busy at night or get too distracted to organize yourself after leaving school, then this is not the strategy for you.

PAPER ORGANIZATION STRATEGY #4:

Sort papers you will use later and papers you can get rid of because they are no longer needed. Strategy # 4 is the simplest, but you need to take extra time at home to make it really work. All you need is a folder with two pockets (one on each side). Put papers to keep at home (papers you will need later) on one side and papers that you can get rid of on the other. You can mark one side "KEEP" or "FILE" and the other side "RECYCLE" or "TRASH."

During the school day, you would put any papers that you need to keep on the "KEEP" side, and papers that can get tossed would go on the "RECYCLE" side. Then, either when you get home from school or on the weekend, you would take all the papers in the "RECYCLE" side and get rid of them. (You might want to show your parents your work first.) Papers that you need to keep—like study notes or completed assignments, can be moved to a folder at home. You might want to have more than one folder to keep your "KEEP" papers organized.

If you use this strategy, you don't end up carrying around papers that you don't need in your backpack. Rosie found this strategy helpful. She said, "I never used to empty out any papers from my folders. The problem was that my folders were overstuffed by November! It feels so good to clean stuff out. Truthfully, I only do this about once every other week, but it's a great tip!"

Organize Your Computer Files

Many students use laptops or iPads for note-taking and homework. However, just like it's harder to find your notes if you just throw them all inside your backpack, if you just put all your computer files into one folder, it's harder to access them when you need them.

Naming your digital files with the subject and date (like "readingnotes_oct31," "readingnotes_nov7," "readingbooksummary_1," and "readingbooksummary_2") and arranging those files inside folders with subject names (like "English," "Math," and "Spanish") are great ways to organize and locate materials. Amy came up with an even more detailed system. She explained "I had three social studies file folders named 'SocialStudies_13colonies,' 'SocialStudies_immigration,' and 'SocialStudies_native americans.' One for each of the major topic areas for the year. This way, it was easier to keep everything simple and clear for myself."

Remember to Bring Home the Right Materials

Bringing home the right books is more complicated than it sounds. Think about the steps involved:

1 Remember the homework you need to do for each class;

2 Know what books you need to do the homework;

3 Find the books you need;

4 Find the folders or other materials you need;

5 Put them in your backpack.

It might sound easy when you read the steps, but it's not always easy to do. Imagine it's the end of the day. You get a chance to make plans for the weekend with your friend Seth. He's packing up, so you go over to him and start talking. Soon, everyone is leaving school and you haven't even packed up. Yikes! So, you just throw everything you can see into your backpack. This might sometimes work, but you may end up missing some of the materials you need for your homework.

HOMEWORK PLANNING STRATEGY #1:

Keep a list of your assignments in one homework pad. Even though you may have different binders or folders for each subject, consider having only one homework organizer or calendar. Take it with you to each class or have it handy for each subject. Maybe have a separate place in your backpack for it, so you can always easily grab it. Write every assignment in it. This way, you just look over the homework organizer at the end of the day, take the books, folders, or notebooks that you need to complete each assignment, put them in your bag, and go! This strategy can also work if you are a student who prefers to keep everything organized electronically. For example, if you have a smartphone, you can type your homework assignments into your notepad (if this is okay with your teachers) and check it at the end of the day so you know what to pack up.

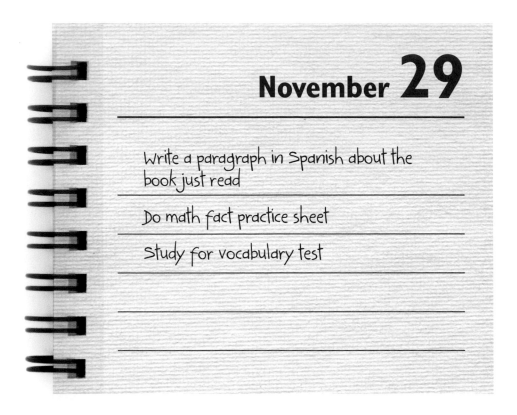

November **29**

Write a paragraph in Spanish about the book just read

Do math fact practice sheet

Study for vocabulary test

HOMEWORK PLANNING STRATEGY #2:

Use a checklist. Some kids like using homework checklists. You may find them helpful too. You can even make your own checklist. All you need to do is create a five-column table on a sheet of paper with your subjects listed at the top, such as "SPANISH, MATH, SCIENCE, SOCIAL STUDIES, ENGLISH." Maybe type the subjects in large print. Then make a lot of copies of the checklist. Each school day you would use one blank checklist, and after each class write down any assignments or reminders under each subject. For example, you might write something like "study for vocabulary test" under "ENGLISH," or "do math fact practice sheet" under "MATH," or "write a paragraph in Spanish about the book just read" under "SPANISH." At the end of each day, review your checklist and check off each homework

Homework checklist

SPANISH	MATH	SCIENCE	SOCIAL STUDIES	ENGLISH
Write a paragraph in Spanish about the book just read	Do math fact practice			Study for vocabulary test

assignment after you put the needed materials to do it in your back-pack or bag. You might want to put an extra check just before you put the assignment checklist into your backpack. So, the check marks mean that you have:

1) put everything you need to do your homework in your backpack before you leave school, and
2) put your homework assignments in your backpack.

Katie tried using a checklist and reported, "I finally found a system that worked for me. My friends saw my checklist and started using it too. I don't have to ask my parents to drive me back to school so I can get my homework or books anymore. I haven't missed an assignment yet!"

Make a "To-Do" and "Done" folder. Another strategy is to keep a two-pocket folder for all your homework and assignments. One side of the folder is labeled "TO DO" and the other side is labeled "DONE." At the end of the day, look through the "TO DO" pocket and make sure you have everything you need in order to do your work—books, files, notebooks. Once you have completed the homework, move it to the "DONE" side of the folder so you can turn it in to your teacher the next day.

It's okay to ask your teacher to explain a lesson. The teacher may see your questions as a sign of your interest!

Understand the Homework Assignments Before Leaving School

Justin cautions other kids, "Just because you have the right books doesn't mean you'll get your homework done. I used to be so happy to get out of class that I never asked my teacher questions that I had about doing the work. So, once I got home, I still didn't understand what to do. My bad!"

As Justin learned, it's hard to do your homework when you don't understand it. If this has ever happened to you, consider one of these tips:

- Raise your hand during class to ask questions so you understand the work. (Other kids may learn from the answer too!)

- After the lesson, ask your teacher to explain the homework again if you don't understand.

- If there is no time after class to talk to the teacher, ask your teacher if you can come back later or right after school to talk about your questions.

- Talk to a friend in the class or an older sibling who has taken the class before. They may be able to explain the assignment to you.

Step 2: Preparation

You've read about where to put your papers, class notes, and assignments; how to make sure you bring home the right materials; and how to get answers to your questions about the homework before leaving school. It's now time to learn about pre-studying preparation at home.

First, a reminder: When it comes to studying, you want to make sure that your body is well rested and well nourished. That means that you get enough sleep and have a well-balanced diet. You may want to re-read the tips for eating healthy and getting enough sleep in Chapter 2. When your body is taken care of, it's easier to think clearly. To get into the study mindset, you may also need to think about your emotions. Remember reading about this? Are you angry about doing the work? Are you nervous about whether you can do it? If you are feeling emotionally tense or upset, try using some of the relaxation techniques that you learned about in Chapter 2.

Now, let's look at some ways to prepare yourself for studying. It's important to figure out the best time and place for you to study and to make sure that you have the supplies you need. Setting up a "study zone" and creating an environment where you can be productive will make it easier to focus on your homework. Here's how to begin:

TOOL KIT FOR PREPARING TO STUDY

- **Find your best time to study**
- **Choose a good place to study**
- **Figure out the best time to take breaks**
- **Take books out of your backpack**
- **Start with the right "stuff"**

Find Your Best Time to Study

Think about what would work best for you. Here are some things to consider:

- What other activities do you have before and after school?
- When are you best able to concentrate?
- When will you have enough time to study?

These three questions are a good place to start. Eddie found, "I play sports and I'm in some after-school clubs, so I would never have time to study right after school. I'm tired when I get home. I'm also starving. I'm a night owl and my home is quiet at night, so I try to do my homework after dinner. This works, but sometimes I don't finish it all and I know I still have a little time in the morning to do it."

What time works for you? You may need to be flexible sometimes, but it's good to know what your general studying schedule will look like. Your parents can help you figure out the time that also works best with your family responsibilities and other activities. You can also think about when you have the most energy during the week for studying. Brian had fewer activities after school on Tuesdays and Wednesdays, so he put more time into studying and doing his homework on those nights. If you always wake up early, maybe you can block off time in the morning to review material for tests or do assignments that are due later in the week. Morning, though, is usually not the best time for studying new material or doing homework due that day because you may run out of time if you sleep late or something unexpected happens that keeps you from concentrating on your work.

You've learned about ways to keep track of your assignments, and you figured out a good time to study. Now, try to stick to your plan. If you have a predictable, manageable schedule, then you may feel less overwhelmed with all of your school responsibilities and better able to focus on what you have to do.

There is no one best time to study. Find the time that works best for you.

	MONDAY	TUESDAY	WEDNESDAY	THURSDAY	FRIDAY
3:00 pm					
3:30 pm	band practice		band practice	homework	
4:00 pm				homework	
4:30 pm					
5:00 pm	homework	homework			Time to organize stuff from week
5:30 pm	homework	homework	homework		
6:00 pm			homework		
6:30 pm	Soccer practice			Soccer practice	
7:00 pm					
7:30 pm		homework	homework		
8:00 pm					
8:30 pm	reading	reading	reading	reading	
9:00 pm	lights out	lights out	lights out	lights out	lights out

Choose a Good Place to Study

So, you know when you want to study and do your homework, but where should you do it? Lots of kids find that they do their homework every day at the kitchen table or in their room at their desk. Having a dedicated study spot can really help you focus and get your work done. You don't have to use the same study spot for all your work, though. You may find that it is helpful to study the same subject in the same place most of the time. For example, Ruth always studied her math at the kitchen table with her mom nearby, so her mom could help her when she was confused. She did her writing assignments on the computer in the family office because it was the quietest place in the house. She did all other work in her bedroom at her desk. She saved her reading assignments for later and read in bed.

There are many places to study. You just need to find what works for you! Some schools set aside time in an after-school program or after lunch where kids can complete some or all of their homework. Some kids ask their parents to take them to the library to do their homework so that there are no distractions. Others, like Ruth, find study spots at home. Think about where you like to do your work and feel most productive, and then check with your parents to see if your study place works for them too. You don't want to pick the family room as the place to do all your work when your brother usually hangs out there with his friends before dinner, or the family office if your mom will be using the computer.

Figure Out the Best Time to Take Breaks

Now that you've found a good place to study, it's time to think about how long you can work before you need a break. Oscar found, "If I work for more than half an hour, I get all wiggly and distracted. I feel like I need to run a marathon." Oscar began to plan his study breaks every 30 minutes to avoid feeling "trapped" by his schoolwork. First, he set a timer on his watch for 30 minutes to do homework. Then, after the timer went off, he set the timer for 5 minutes to take a break doing something else—listening to music, tossing a ball, drawing, playing with his dog—anything other than studying.

You might think that taking breaks would extend the amount of time it takes you to do your work, but often it actually makes the work go faster since it helps you focus better. Think about how long you can study before taking a break. Then add five-minute breaks. Be careful not to do something like text your friends, because you will probably need more than five minutes and you may be left thinking about what your friend said when it is time to think about homework.

3:30–3:50 PM:	Snack!
3:50–4:00 PM:	Get out homework/ set up study area
4:00–4:30 PM:	Reading
4:30–4:35 PM:	Break!
4:35–5:05 PM:	Math homework
5:05–5:10 PM:	Break!
5:10–5:40 PM:	Study for social studies test
5:40–5:45 PM:	Break!

Take Books out of Your Backpack

Earlier in this chapter, you learned how to pack up your backpack before leaving school. In order to have all your books ready to go back to school in the morning, try to keep everything in your backpack except for what you are working on at the moment. So, only your math book is out while you are doing math homework. If you immediately put the book back in your backpack after you finish the homework, then you can feel confident that you will have everything you need to bring back to school the next day. You're already packed up for school!

Start With the Right "Stuff"

Before starting your work, make sure you have the pencils, erasers, extra paper, calculator (if you're allowed to use one), rulers, or dictionary that you need to get your assignment done. If you do a lot of work on the computer, take some time to set up bookmarks for websites that you may use when doing your homework. (Your teacher may be able to help you identify useful websites.) If you have to jump out of your seat a couple of times to get things after you start your work, or if you need to ask your mom for materials, you may find that it takes longer to complete homework and you are more distracted. Be prepared with all the things you need, so you can settle down and get to work.

Summary

In this chapter, you read about a lot of tips for getting organized, such as how to put handouts in the right folders and notes in the right notebook, and how to bring home the right materials for your homework. You also had a chance to think about where and when you study best. It can seem really overwhelming to try to manage all of your subjects, but be patient and try the strategies you've learned. If one of the techniques doesn't work for you, try another. Keep trying until you find what works for you!

5.

Executive Functioning Skills for Studying

There are several important skills that make homework and studying easier. These are called executive functioning skills. It's a cool name to throw around: "Mom, I'm busy using my executive functioning skills!" Executive functions are processes in your brain that help you pay attention and get things done. Executive functioning skills include planning, organizing, strategizing, and holding things in your short-term memory. These skills are useful for anyone trying to manage a lot of responsibilities. Before starting, please put a check mark next to the items below that describe how you deal with assignments:

☐ I don't need reminders to get started on my homework.

☐ If I have a lot of homework, I can easily decide what to do first.

☐ I usually make sure that I have enough time to complete my homework.

☐ I am usually calm enough to complete the work without getting upset.

☐ I pay attention to the work in front of me, and don't get distracted.

Wouldn't it be great if you had a coach or cheerleader ready to praise you for the good study habits listed above? Someone who encourages you as

> **Practicing and polishing your executive functioning skills can help make studying less stressful.**

you go through your studying routine? The good news is that you can have a coach and cheerleader. It is YOU!

Using your executive functioning skills—and rewarding yourself for it—can make your studying time less stressful. We'll get to the rewards in Chapter 7. For now, let's talk about being your own coach.

In this chapter, we'll cover five major executive functioning skills: initiation, prioritization, time management, emotional control, and focus. You actually learned about two executive functioning skills in Chapter 4: organization and preparation. Organization and preparation are the first two essential steps before starting on your assignments or studying.

Let's move onto the next step. The next executive function is *initiation*. Essentially, this step is about getting started studying or doing your homework without feeling overwhelmed.

STEP 3: Initiation

Getting started is often the hardest part. Where do you begin? What is most important? Getting started has a fancy name: *initiation*. Many kids struggle with initiation and end up waiting to begin a project

TOOL KIT FOR USING EXECUTIVE FUNCTIONING SKILLS

- **Get started**
- **Prioritize**
- **Manage your time wisely**
- **Control your emotions**
- **Focus**

until the night before it is due, because they didn't know how to begin or how to motivate themselves to start working.

Initiation is the beginning of your journey toward finishing your work. It doesn't involve studying. It's similar to a baker preheating his oven before he starts baking. It may involve re-reading your assignment so that you know what homework you are going to begin. First, pat yourself on the back for caring and trying to start your work. That wasn't too hard, right? Initiation doesn't have to be hard either.

Now, how to begin? In the last chapter, you picked a place to study, so bring your backpack or books to that place. Try following these steps:

Getting started is often a difficult step, so congratulate yourself for doing it!

1. Put everything on the table or desk, so that you can see the work that you need to do.

2. Re-read your assignments to be sure you understand the instructions.

3. Double-check that you have the right books and notes.

4. Make sure that you have the pencil, pen, or computer that you will need.

Four easy steps. Once you have started by looking at your homework pad and getting your materials together, you have finished Step 3! Now it's time to get to Step 4.

STEP 4: Prioritization

In Step 3 you simply brought your materials to your study place and looked at your homework papers. Now, it's time to prioritize. *Prioritization* is the process of figuring out which part of your homework to begin with and what is most important to finish. An artist starting a landscape painting has to decide whether to begin with a pencil sketch, watercolors, or oils, and whether to start with the trees, ocean, or sky. Similarly, you have to make decisions on what to focus on for your school work, when to focus on it, and how to do it.

Does prioritizing sound complicated? It really just means figuring out in what order to do your work and where to start. Take a look at your homework and think about how you would like to do the work. You can even rank the assignments and number them in your homework checklist or organizer so that you know in what order you will focus on your work.

There is no one right way to do this. Some kids always put easy work first, so they get it over with and feel like they accomplished something. Other kids like to do the work that takes the most concentration first when they are feeling most relaxed and ready. David had a different strategy. "I took the homework I hated and put a number one next to that. I wanted to finish it and get it over with. Otherwise, I dread it all night." What works for you?

You can try a couple of different systems to find which one you prefer. Like David, you might want to prioritize based on how you feel about the work. Or you might want to put a number one or two next to work that is due the next day and number three or four next to work that is not due for two or three days. But don't forget to do that work too!

What if you have to study for a test or quiz that covers lots of pages in your reading book or many vocab words or math facts? What if you have a huge project that will take several hours (or days) to finish? If you plan ahead, you can make these big assignments smaller. Simply divide the study time or big project into smaller parts and prioritize the parts in the same way you would prioritize your homework assignments. For example, let's say you have a test in 7 days that covers 20 pages in your geography book, and you don't want to study for it over the weekend. That

November 29

1) Write a paragraph in Spanish about the book just read

3) Do math facts practice sheet

2) Study for vocabulary test

means you have four school nights to study. You only need to do ¼ of the studying each night in order to get it done. So, each day you do homework, just add "study for geography test (5 pages)" to your list. You won't feel the pressure of doing it all the night before your test if you prioritize five pages each night. It helps to plan ahead!

One great way to keep track of long-term projects and tests that may be coming up in the next few weeks is to have a calendar that has one large page per month, so you can write in when the assignments are due.

Check out the way Melissa filled out her calendar for March:

MARCH

Su	Mo	Tu	We	Th	Fr	Sa
Week ONE	Do math sheet Write one paragraph essay for English class	Study for short health test	Do 1/5 of DNA project Review studying for health test	Do 1/5 of DNA project Look over spelling words for test next week	Health test	
Week TWO	Do 1/5 of DNA project Learn spelling words for test	Do 1/5 of DNA project Review spelling words for test	Do 1/5 of DNA project Spelling Test	Check DNA project for any errors	DNA project due	
Week THREE	Read 5 pgs of geography book Do math sheet	Read 5 pgs of geography book Look over Spanish vocab words	Read 5 pgs of geography book Practice Spanish vocab words	Read 5 pgs of geography book Review notes on geography reading assignment	Geography test	
Week FOUR	Study for math test Review Spanish vocab words	Review for math test Spanish vocab quiz	Math test	Write up science experiment		

If you look at all the work you need to do, you may want to scream or cry. Emily had fantasies of throwing her books out of her window before she learned about the way to use this calendar. Emily later explained, "I couldn't think about doing all the studying. Luckily, I didn't throw away my books. I never knew that I could do small parts of the work each night and not have to cram. Now that I know how to prioritize, and focus on doing parts of projects or studying instead of all of it at once, it always makes getting started easier. I don't panic anymore!"

Prioritizing is important because it helps you focus on what is important in the short-term, but it is also important to pay attention to the assignments that are not due the next day because they might include tests or projects that will have a big impact on your report card grade.

Now that you know about prioritizing, it's time to move on to Step 5.

STEP 5: Time Management

Time management means figuring out ways to do the things you need (and want) to do every day. Face it, you are probably a busy kid! After school you have to do your homework, but you might also have soccer practice or music lessons. Plus, you probably want to hang out with your friends, watch TV or play video games, have dinner, do your chores, and get enough sleep. How do you get it all done in a day?

First, you have to think about how long it takes to do things. You may not be sure how long it takes you to finish 2 math pages or to read 30 pages of your science book. So you need to act like a scientist or detective and collect data by timing yourself (without rushing) and then determine when you can fit everything in to your daily schedule.

Here's a step-by-step plan:

1 Make a list of the things you want to be able to do after school.

2 Prioritize the order that you plan to do them.

3 Time yourself doing each thing on a few nights. How long does it usually take you to do your math homework? Eat dinner? Do your chores?

4 How many hours do you have after school and before you go to sleep to fit in activities?

5 If you want to do so many things that you run out of time, is there something you can do more quickly? For example, could you spend less time texting friends? Or could you record a favorite television show and watch it during the weekend when you have more time? Be creative.

6 Decide what activities you can't do more quickly and still do them well, such as writing an essay for English class. Mark these tasks as high priorities and figure out if there is a night during the week when you have more time and can focus more intensively on these.

After doing your detective work, let's say you have figured out that it takes you 10 minutes to do your math worksheet, 15 minutes to write your vocabulary sentences, and 35 minutes to read two short chapters of your reading book. That's an hour of work. So, if you get home from school at 4:00pm, eat dinner at 6:00pm, and go to soccer practice at 7:30pm, when will you do your homework? (Hint: Sometime between getting home and dinner, maybe 5–6:00pm?) But what do you do if you have more work than you have time to do? Let's say you have one hour before soccer practice and 30 minutes after practice before you need to shower and go to bed. You have two hours of homework. Can you do all your work? Do you need to start studying earlier from now on? Is there time at school during lunch or recess that you could squeeze in a little work? Can you do a little bit of homework in the morning before leaving for school? There is no right answer here. But if you figure out how long it takes to complete your homework, you will probably be able to find time to get it all done. Finishing all your work and not getting too stressed are the goals.

Ray paid attention to how long it took him to do his work. He explained, "My English papers always took a long time for me. I'm not fast at thinking of my ideas and writing them down. I also have to always remember to double-check what I wrote. So, I learned that I have to start my homework a little early on days when I have to write a paper. I hate losing time relaxing and hanging out with friends, but I know I get embarrassed and stressed when my teacher points out that I didn't finish my work."

When you have to study for a big test or finish a research paper, you may want to plan more time for your school work and less time for videogames or other activities. Remember that there will be other days when you need less time for homework and you can spend more time on other things!

Now, you have initiated your work (started to focus on it), prioritized it (determined the order in which you will do the work), and completed your time management plan (figured how much time you will spend doing the work). Congratulate yourself! You are almost ready to do your work. There are only two more steps to get through.

STEP 6: Emotional Control

Athletes need to learn to manage their emotions if they want to excel. A manager or coach wants to make sure that the player will handle directions and follow rules, even if the player is unhappy with them. Imagine if a basketball player got upset and pushed a ref for making a call that the player didn't like. If this player really let his emotions get out of control, and got physical with the ref, you can bet that he'd face consequences (sometimes known as penalties). It's not always easy to be in control of your emotions, but it's like any other exercise—it takes practice! Remember reading about Emily? She wanted to throw her books out of the window because she was upset that she had so much homework and didn't know how to handle it. This step is about coming up with ways to keep calm while doing work. In Chapter 2, you read about relaxation techniques. Now is a good time to review them—before starting your homework.

What happens if you were confused about your social studies assignment in school today and have no idea how to do the homework? If you feel overwhelmed or frustrated, you might scream, think about how much you hate your teacher, convince yourself that you are "stupid," or cry. As you know, though, these reactions don't solve the problem.

Having emotional control means that you have developed the confidence to handle tricky situations—like being confused by assignments—without having meltdowns. Next time, you may want to ask questions about the lesson or assignment before leaving school. But what do you do tonight?

Here are some tips for handling confusion:

- Read any explanations that are on the handout from the teacher.

- Look at the textbook and see if certain words are explained.

- Call a friend who has the same teacher or takes the same subject.

- E-mail your teacher and ask for extra help.

- Plan to finish the work you do understand and then talk to your teacher before class to explain that you wanted to do the work but needed help.

It is easier to stay in control of your emotions when you eat well and get enough sleep. Also, remind yourself that you do not have to be perfect when you do your school work. You would already be in college if you knew everything from middle school and high school.

Sometimes you can psych yourself into feeling like the work is too hard for you. Remember:

- Using phrases like "I can't get this" or "I'm stupid" only keep you from having the confidence to try.

- Rather than saying, "I can't," think of the story about the Little Engine Who Could, and say, "I think I can." Try it, really. The words we use can change our thinking and our feelings.

- The more confident you are in believing you can handle the work, the less stressful the experience may be.

At times, you may even feel like homework is fun and you can stay positive while doing the work. It's okay to admit to feeling annoyed or frustrated at other times, as long as it doesn't hurt you. It hurt Stephen even though he didn't get down on himself. "I blamed my teacher for making me do so much work at home. So, I wanted to get back at him and I decided not to do any of his assignments. What a bad idea! I lost my chance to sing in the select chorus and my parents were really upset with my grades. The truth is that I was just scared that I wouldn't be able to do the work. I didn't do the work and I failed. Great strategy . . . NOT!"

Avoiding homework and the stress it might cause you can feel pretty good at first. However, the panic that sets in when you are supposed to hand in the assignment isn't worth feeling good for that short period of time. Have you ever experienced this conflict about whether to avoid or do the work? A lot of kids struggle with this. How do you motivate yourself to get started? You may feel better about starting your work when you realize that Steps 1-6 (and even Step 7) can be done in about ten minutes!

Remember that you can be your own coach and you can motivate yourself!

STEP 7: Focus

Executives need to focus on important issues and responsibilities. Imagine if an employee told the boss that there was a gas smell in the basement of the office building and the executive said he'd look into it, but he was actually thinking about going on vacation and didn't follow up. If this executive couldn't focus on what the employee said, and never looked into this smell, it could become a very serious problem.

Focusing means paying attention to the task at hand, and not getting distracted by other thoughts. For example, focusing means

KIDS' QUESTIONS ANSWERED!

Mindy's Question: **I love cooking and want to be a chef. Why do I have to go to school?**

A lot of people feel like it would be great just to do things that they love, all day long. However, school can help kids learn executive functioning skills needed for many jobs. So, if you want to be a chef, think about what school can teach you. In school you can learn:

- to follow a schedule (organizational skills)

- how to handle many tasks (prioritizing)

- how to meet deadlines (time management)

- how to deal with pressure (emotional control)

- the math and reading abilities that you need to follow recipes

- to work as a member of a team

You may be able to add to this list. For example, school can even give you more information about other job choices. You may decide to switch careers and have cooking as a hobby. School also allows you to be with other kids your age, maybe play a sport, or be in a school play. Try to keep this in mind when you feel annoyed about having to be in school.

that when it's time to study, you pay attention to what you are reading rather than thinking about your best friend's birthday party. Focusing can make your studying, and your social life, easier to manage.

How can you stop thinking about other things when it's time to study? Some kids have found the following strategies helpful:

- Make a list of things you want to do when you finish studying, so you don't forget, then put it aside.

- Change rooms. Pick a new room where you can do your work more easily because you have fewer distractions.

- Put on calming music to block out other noises in your home.

- Know your best time to study (when you are most alert and can focus best).

Focusing also means that you pay attention to details, so you can complete your assignments correctly. For example, if you're focused on your teacher's instructions for your essay assignment, you won't write about the wrong topic. Other important details to focus on include: how long an essay is supposed to be; whether you need to show your math work on the homework sheet; and the due date for a project. Do you need to add a bibliography to your social studies paper? How do you keep track of whether you really completed each part of your assignment?

Brittany came up with a strategy for making sure she focused on completing all of her work. "I put each assignment on a separate piece of scrap paper. When I finished the work for that assignment, I would double-check that I did all the parts of the work, then I'd crumble the scrap paper into a ball and toss it into the recycling bin. I love sports, especially basketball, so this was like a little fun after I finished work for each teacher. When all the scraps when in the recycling bin, I knew I was done."

Getting your work done and getting it done correctly are two different things. Make sure you double-check your homework to make sure you did everything you needed to do. Did you answer all the questions? Did you use proper punctuation? Did you write in complete sentences? Do you have your name and the date on the top of the page? You can even build in a system for double-checking that you did all your homework. For example, you can cross off each item on your homework checklist after you've double-checked it. Or, you can put a smiley face next to each item in your homework pad once you have double-checked it and finished it entirely.

Joey took some of his three-year-old brother's stickers (with permission!) and put one sticker on a piece of paper each time he completed a homework item and double-checked that it was done. He decided he would make the stickers into a picture of a lacrosse stick, which made doing the work, and finishing it, more fun! What works for you?

Summary

In this chapter, you learned about some of the important executive functioning skills—initiation, prioritization, time management, emotional control, and focus. You may even want to share these skills with family members during dinner. You can tell your family that you are going to start using some of the skills, like initiating, prioritizing, managing your time, staying cool, and maybe even being more focused.

You are now on your way to knowing how to juggle your responsibilities without feeling like you want to rip the hair out of your head. You have learned that it is worth taking some time to use executive functioning techniques before even starting an assignment. Keep using all of these skills and you may find that your academic muscles will get stronger with practice!

In the next two chapters, you will learn some study strategies that have helped other kids. Learning how to study is like learning how to dance, or throw a football, or any other skill. There are ways to build up your academic skills so you feel more confident in your abilities.

6.

Time Management Tricks for Getting Your Work Done

At this point, you have read about how to figure out what causes you stress and you have learned some stress-busting strategies to deal with it. You have also learned how to use executive functioning skills to be your own coach. Do you remember reading about time management in Chapter 5? Time management skills are talked about in a variety of sections in this book because using time wisely can decrease anxiety and help you decide what you can or cannot do on a particular day.

In this chapter, you'll learn some more tips for managing your time so you can get your homework done.

Before starting this chapter, put a check mark next to the strategies listed below that you feel comfortable using:

☐ I know how to use my time wisely, even when I'm on the internet.

☐ I plan ahead so I never have to cram to finish my long-term projects.

☐ I take the time to make sure my work is neat and there are no spelling errors.

How many of these items did you check off? Even if you already know some ways to manage your time and get all your homework done, this chapter may even give you more ideas.

Using Time Wisely

It is sometimes difficult to decide when to "play" and when to work. If a friend invites you to join her family on a boat ride, and it's a great afternoon to be outside on the water, how do you decide if you should go? While you need permission from your parents, you also need to decide if you should give yourself permission. If you have a project due the next day, perhaps it would be a better use of your time to stay in and finish your project.

Time management may be even more complicated for your generation than for earlier generations of students because of easy access to the internet and online chats. Sometimes, teachers will ask you to use the internet to do some research or to go to a particular website. At times, group projects are done online as well. The internet makes it faster to do research and find the information you need for your projects, right? Sometimes it does, but sometimes it can actually add some distractions.

The internet has so many interesting sites. Online chats can take interesting turns. Group projects can quickly become group gossip time. You want to fit in and maybe you are sometimes interested in chatting. You might want to socialize rather than do your work. How do you fight this urge? The truthful answer is that it may not always be easy.

TOOL KIT FOR MANAGING TIME WISELY

- Set aside a certain amount of time
- Work first, then socialize
- Work off-line
- Schedule time to hang out with friends

Adults may say that you need to balance immediate gratification with delayed gratification. Immediate gratification comes from getting what you want right then (chatting with your friends), while delayed gratification comes from meeting your long-term goal (feeling happy and relieved that you finished the project or homework assignment).

Read on to find some ways to balance your online social and study time.

Set Aside a Certain Amount of Time

Maria uses this strategy. She explained, "Before I go onto the internet, I figure out how much time I can spend on the assignment before having to go to swim practice, eat dinner, or finish other work. My swim coach let me have one of his timers. I set it when I use the computer. If I have 30 minutes to work on a certain homework assignment on the computer, and I think the work will take me about 20 minutes, then I figure I can socialize for a few minutes and still get the homework done. This works, except sometimes I admit that I am too interested in the conversation to sign off. But I'm usually pretty good. One of my friends thanked me for signing off one day because she was not getting her work done either. Try the time plan. It's really good."

For Steven, the problem wasn't chatting with friends, it was getting caught up with other interesting websites when he was trying to do his work. He explained, "I would start out researching my paper but then I wanted to see how my favorite sports team did or wanted to look at things I needed for my upcoming camping trip. Before I knew it, I had spent 5 minutes on my work and 40 minutes looking up everything else. I tried Maria's strategy of putting a timer on when I went on a fun website. When the alarm went off, I put the website in 'my favorites' so I could look at it another time and I got back to work. She is right! It really works!"

Work First, Then Socialize

You may want to have fun with friends or family before settling down to do work. Or you might feel that it's rude to tell friends or family that you don't have time to socialize. The problem is that socializing first can lead to you feeling stressed if you run out of time to do the work that is due the next day. Fortunately, there are ways to help your friends understand that you are not being rude by not chatting, but you need to get your work done.

Michael said, "I did all my work that I could do without the computer. Then, I went online. I felt like I needed to see what was happening with my friends, so I did. But I only said a quick 'Hi,' then told them I'd catch them later if I had time after doing my work. I did my group project with other kids and kept trying to convince them that we needed to get the work done before just video-chatting. One day, a friend started saying, 'yes, sir!' to me. That was kind of annoying. But once we finished the work and started hanging, he even admitted that I was right."

One tip that Abby offered is to "set an away message. You can usually do this on your instant messaging. I use this so my friends know I can't chat right then. As soon as I'm done with my online work for school, I change this setting so my friends know I'm available. It's an easy way to let everyone know when I can and when I can't hang with them online."

Work Off-Line

There may be some nights when you really do not need the computer to do your homework. On these nights, try to use the computer as your reward after getting your work done.

Schedule Time to Hang out With Friends

When it comes to hanging with friends in person, the same time management skills are important. Figure out how long you need to get your work done and how much free time you have, then see if there is

KIDS' QUESTIONS ANSWERED!

Kanye's Question: **I'm doing a lot of fun things, but have no time for me. How can I get more time for me?**

Life can be very interesting when you find a lot of fun activities to do. However, sometimes kids get overwhelmed and exhausted trying to fit too much into each day.

Here are some things to keep in mind:

- First of all, think about your schedule. Can you do the art club in the fall, then a winter sport, then join the photography club in the spring?

- Sometimes, kids can do many activities, just not all at once.

- Learning the skills for prioritizing and time management may allow you to find time for yourself.

- Think about how much "me time" you want and try to schedule it into your calendar.

If you don't have enough "me time," it's time to re-think your schedule.

enough free time to get together and socialize with your friends. Remember to factor in after-school activities, dinner with your family, time to do your chores, and so forth. If your friends want to hang out, but you don't have enough time, make a plan to get together with them that weekend, or whenever you will be free, as a reward to yourself for getting your work done.

Managing Short-Term and Long-Term Projects

When trying to figure out what to do each night, remember one of the tips you read about in the last chapter: In addition to assignments that are due the next day, you need to factor in time to do a little of your long-term projects each night, so you don't end up doing everything at the last minute.

One great tip was offered by Jeremy. He said, "I use math to figure out how to do long-term projects. I divide the project into small steps and figure out how many steps are needed to finish it. I want each step to be about only 15 minutes. This way, it doesn't take a lot of time at night. I then make a ladder with the number of 15-minute steps and color in each step when I'm done. When I get to the top of the ladder, I reward myself." (Chapter 7 discusses some ways to reward yourself.) An example of how Jeremy divided up his steps is shown on the next page. Jeremy shows how he prepared to give an oral report to his class about the life of one of his sports heroes.

Using Jeremy's strategy, you can also plan when you will do each step. If you have a month-at-a-glance calendar, and you know that you need ten steps to do the project, pick dates on your calendar to do each step (along with your nightly homework). If you know that you have more time on Monday, Tuesday, and Thursday afternoons, then try adding the project to these dates until it's done. (See page 90 for an example of how Jeremy scheduled each step.) Remember, each step only takes a little time each day.

Jeremy's Project

Ready to give presentation in class!

10. Practice oral report in front of mirror, using pictures from poster board to show him at different stages of life.

9. Print out pictures from internet of the guy and put them on poster board.

8. Write what makes this guy special (1–2 index cards).

7. Write about his professional sports life— teams, stats (1–2 index cards).

6. Write how he got into the pros and about his personality (1–2 index cards).

5. Write paragraph on the guy's childhood (1–2 index cards).

4. Continue reading about the guy.

3. Read the material printed out from Step 2 and look through books from Step 1.

2. Search the internet for information— childhood, personality, sports stats.

1. Decide who I will write about & go to library to check out books on him.

Su	Mo	Tu	We	Th	Fr	Sa
	Step 1	Step 2		Step 3		
	Step 4	Step 5		Step 6		
	Step 7	Step 8		Step 9		
	Step 10 of project (REWARD MYSELF!!)				Project due date	

Presentation of Work

As you are writing your research paper, or completing your homework, take some time to think about how your work looks. Even if you put a lot of time into your work, if it is presented in a sloppy way or on crumpled paper, your teacher may think that you did not care about the assignment. Your teacher may even think that you don't care about the class.

Mrs. Gold, who teaches social studies, reported, "I always tell my students to take pride in their work. If it looks sloppy, then I don't think they really cared as much as they should have about doing it."

Stacey knew that the way her papers looked could affect how her teacher viewed her. She fell into a different trap, though. Stacey explained, "I made sure my school work was neat and that my spelling was good. But I hate writing long papers and thought I found a way around it. When my English teacher asked for a two page paper about a book, I did a two page paper. I used a large font and made my margins a little bigger than normal. This way, I didn't need to write as many words. It seemed like a great plan until my teacher called me on it. I felt really embarrassed. Now I realize that my teacher felt I was cheating. I think I was too, but I wasn't trying to do anything wrong." You can learn from Stacey's experience.

Before handing in your work, it is helpful to think about the way your work looks. Take a minute to double-check the following items:

- The paper is neat and not crumpled, ripped, or torn.
- Your handwriting is legible and neat.
- Your font size and margins are acceptable to your teacher.
- You have no spelling errors or typos.
- You answered the question fully and did the right assignment.

Work that is neatly presented will give others the impression that you cared about the assignment.

Summary

In this chapter, you learned some ways to balance friendships with schoolwork, as well as ways to plan for short-term and long-term projects. In addition, this chapter reviewed why the presentation of your work can effect a teacher's impression of you and the completed assignment. In the next chapter, you will learn about even more study strategies so that you can choose from a variety of plans to deal with your school work.

7.

Homework and Studying Tips

This chapter focuses on study techniques. If you find a strategy that works for you, it can even be fun to use! Take a minute to check off any of these techniques or strategies that you use already:

☐ I know my learning style and study based on my learning style.

☐ I am really good at making up sentences or words to remind myself of information that I have to remember (mnemonics).

☐ I quiz myself on the material by using flashcards, online games, or creating my own quiz game.

☐ I like to teach others about what I'm studying.

☐ I make studying a game by setting a timer and racing against the clock.

☐ I draw flow charts, webs, or maps to organize my thoughts.

☐ I highlight or take notes to remember important material.

☐ I match my study strategy to the format of the test.

☐ I practice oral reports in front of the mirror.

☐ I usually avoid cramming for tests.

☐ I reward myself for finishing difficult (or boring) work.

☐ I sometimes think of creative ways to do my projects.

If you checked off some of the items on the previous page, then you already know some strategies for studying that hopefully help you. The more study techniques that you are comfortable using, the easier it will be to pick a strategy to fit different assignments. Matching your studying methods to your learning style can help. So, what is your learning style? The next section will help you answer this question.

Learning Styles

The five basic senses help us to learn and remember—hearing, sight, touch, smell, and taste. While smell and taste can help you remember a vacation (e.g., the taste of good food, or the smell of the salt air at the beach), hearing, sight, and touch can be more easily used for doing your school work. These are called auditory (hearing), visual (sight), and kinesthetic (touch) learning styles, respectively.

If you know which senses you learn best through, you can use this knowledge to help you study. Below are examples of ways that auditory, visual, and kinesthetic learners can use their learning styles to help them study.

Auditory Learner

Auditory learners are comfortable learning new information by listening and speaking. So, if you are an auditory learner, use this skill to your advantage when studying. Read your material aloud so that you hear the words as you do your homework. Saying the material over and over is more likely to make the information stick with you. Some students like to record their voices when they are studying or reading. They can then listen to it later when it comes closer to test time.

Have fun with your learning style and make up a song with the information you need. Try to take the beat from your favorite song and put in your own lyrics to summarize your study material. Sarah loved opera and did a dramatic song about the struggles of young soldiers fighting in the Civil War and the sadness of their families when the men were killed. Steve loved rap and wrote a rap about DNA and the parts of the cell. Steve even got his friends to learn the song and they all felt it helped them pass the test! Of course, a single song is probably not the total studying package, but it is one way that you can increase your chances of memorizing material.

Visual Learner

Visual learners prefer to look at material, or read it, to remember. So, if you are a visual learner, read and re-read! Maybe, if you love art, you could draw a picture of the characters in a book that you are discussing in class. If you draw key figures or main characters, you may remember them better (especially if you are both a visual and a kinesthetic learner—you look at the drawings and actively move your hand while drawing). Use some imagination here. For example, if you know that one of the characters in the book wasn't seeing the true problems in his family, then draw the person without eyes. This visual picture can help you to remember the material.

If you need to remember a list of random words, make them visual and meaningful. For instance, you can remember "table," "monkey," and "tree" by picturing the monkey climbing onto the table, then leaping toward the tree. This trick can really help in science, when you have to remember the properties of certain things, such as water. Water is comprised of two hydrogen atoms for every one oxygen atom. So, Jose pictured one oxygen guy dancing with two hydrogen girls. Find what works for you.

Kinesthetic Learner

Kinesthetic learners learn by touching and doing. They often find that they learn best while moving. If this describes you, then think about ways you can adjust your studying so it's more natural for you. Max found a way that worked for him. He explained, "I'm okay about sitting still in class, but I found a good way to memorize stuff at home. When the weather's good, I shoot baskets with my brother. My brother tells me a spelling word and I get to shoot a hoop if I spell it right. Otherwise, he gets the ball and I have to give him a math problem for him to solve before he shoots. We almost don't feel like we're studying, but we learn the stuff quicker this way!"

Another study strategy that helps kinesthetic learners is rewriting notes. The process of writing and rewriting your notes may help you to remember more.

No matter what kind of learner you are, sometimes a combination of strategies works the best. In the next section you will find more techniques so that you can continue to add to your tool kit.

Study Techniques

There are many different study techniques to help you remember information. There is no one right way to study. Try some of these strategies to find what works best for you!

TOOL KIT FOR STUDYING EFFECTIVELY

- Make up mnemonics
- Quiz yourself
- Teach others
- Race against the clock
- Create graphic organizers
- Highlight important material
- Take notes
- Match your study plan to the test format
- Practice in front of the mirror
- Avoid cramming
- Reward yourself!

Make Up Mnemonics

A mnemonic is a fancy word that basically means a "word code" to help you remember things. Imagine trying to accept an Academy Award and having some easy ways to remember the list of people you want to thank. It really can be quite useful!

There are lots of different ways to use words to help your memory. Mnemonics can be used for studying most subjects. You can have fun creating your own, but let's first look at some mnemonics that have been used a lot over the years.

Make up funny sentences. Sometimes people make up funny sentences to help them remember a list of things. The first letter in each word is their key to remembering. For example, have you ever heard the sentence "Please Excuse My Dear Aunt Sally?" Each word starts with a capital letter, because that is the key letter to remember. This sentence actually allows you to remember the order in which to complete algebraic math problems. The order of the steps is: "Parentheses, Exponents, Multiplication, Division, Addition, Subtraction." Do you see how each of the first letters in the sentence matches the first letter in the math operation? It's much harder (and less fun) to just remember the order of the operations without the silly sentence.

Let's pretend that your English teacher asked you to memorize the following list of authors: Shakespeare, Dickinson, Hemingway, and Fitzgerald. Can you think of a sentence that is easy to remember and can trigger your memory? You want a sentence that has four words starting with S, D, H, and F. It can be any sentence you want. Here's an example: "Sam's Dog Has Fur." Are you getting the hang of it?

Create phrases or poems. Another mnemonic device that may work for you is to remember phrases that guide you in approaching your work. Here are just a few:

- a spelling tip: to spell "friend," remember that you can be friends to the end ("friend" ends with the word "end").

- another spelling tip that usually works: remember "I before E, except after C."

- a history tip: "Columbus discovered America in 1492, and I discovered a good friend when I discovered you," or "In 1492, Columbus sailed the ocean blue."

Create an acronym. Sometimes you can make an acronym—a word created from the first letters of a phrase or set of words. For example, "NEWS" can help you remember the four basic directions (north, east, west, south). Do you remember learning "ROY G. BIV" to help you remember the colors of the rainbow? That's an acronym as well. Can you think of other acronyms?

In addition to mnemonics, there are other study strategies you can use to help you remember information.

Quiz Yourself

Quizzing yourself is a great way to learn the material you're studying. You'll be learning the material when you write the questions, and reinforcing that knowledge when you use those questions to quiz yourself. It can also be fun! Here are some ideas for ways to test your knowledge.

Play a game of *Jeopardy*. Have you ever watched *Jeopardy*? In this show, contestants must quickly give the question that goes along with the answer. For example, if the answer is "Father of Psychology," the contestant might accurately respond with the question, "Who was Sigmund Freud?"

You can make your own *Jeopardy* board based on the material you need to study (see page 100). Becca tried this strategy and found, "While I was preparing the game board, I was actually studying." You can put down easy and hard questions and give them point values. You could ask a parent to quiz you, or ask a classmate to play the game with you and come up with some fun prizes!

KIDS' QUESTIONS ANSWERED!

Elizabeth's Question: **Studying is so boring. Is there any way to make it less painful?**

Elizabeth, unfortunately, students need to memorize certain facts, such as multiplication tables. Sometimes this can be boring. Fortunately, there are ways to make this memorization and studying fun. You may want to try:

- creating flashcards and playing the game of Concentration or Jeopardy to learn facts

- making up fun mnemonics to remember information

- making up a song to help you recall facts

- racing against the clock to make studying into a game

- asking a friend how she survives studying.

If you find that studying is boring because it's really just confusing and difficult, try asking your teacher for help. When the work isn't overwhelming, you may find that it's also more interesting.

Category: HEALTH

EXERCISE	NUTRITION	DISEASES	STAYING SAFE AND HEALTHY
100 POINTS	**100 POINTS**	**100 POINTS**	**100 POINTS**
Two positive ways exercise helps your heart	The food group a tomato belongs in	Two names of diseases that affect the lungs where you have trouble breathing	Two ways to cut down your chance of getting diabetes
200 POINTS	**200 POINTS**	**200 POINTS**	**200 POINTS**
Three ways exercise helps your mind	Three foods that are high in calcium	The name of the disease where your body has trouble using insulin	The amount of sleep you should be getting every night
300 POINTS	**300 POINTS**	**300 POINTS**	**300 POINTS**
The amount of calories you need to burn to lose a pound	Five healthy sources of protein	The system that protects your body from disease	The minimum number of SPF you should wear to be safe from the sun
400 POINTS	**400 POINTS**	**400 POINTS**	**400 POINTS**
The meaning of BMI	The difference between saturated and unsaturated fats	The names of two cells that fight infection	Three activities where you should wear a helmet in order to stay safe
500 POINTS	**500 POINTS**	**500 POINTS**	**500 POINTS**
The difference between anaerobic and aerobic exercise	The reason your body needs fiber	The names of two microbes that can infect the body	Two things you must do if there is a fire in your home

Make flashcards. Some people want to skip any discussion about using flashcards to help them study. This strategy has been around a very long time, though, for a reason. It can be very useful for some students, so you might want to give it a try. Write down a question on one side of an index card and the answer on the other. Even just writing the question and answer may help you to remember the information.

Flashcards can be used as a game.

With flashcards, you can randomize the order of the cards (just like your teacher might randomly put questions on the test) so you really get to learn the material. You can also have another person quiz you. They would show you the card, then let you know the right answer if you were confused. Lastly, flashcards allow you to look at the answer and figure out the question or look at the question and figure out the answer.

A great way to make flashcards fun is to play a game of Concentration. Have you ever played this game before with regular playing cards? For the purpose of studying, try writing questions on a card and the answer to that question on another card. Put a code on the two cards (e.g., 'BB') to make sure that you know that the two cards go together. Then, put all the cards on the floor face down. Pick a card. If the answer is "America became independent in this year" then you have to try to match it to the answer (1776). Try it—it really can be fun once you get going. You can play this game alone or with a friend.

Use apps and websites. You may be surprised that some websites and apps have fun games to help you study. There are a number of apps available that allow you to create flashcards on your computer or smartphone. For example, you could go online to Quizlet (www.quizlet .com), and choose from sets of free flashcards, or create your own set.

Some sites are fun but don't help you to learn the material you need for class. Be sure you are using a website or app that's helpful. Ask your teacher for suggestions. For instance, Mr. Kelley often gave his students math websites so that they can practice their long division and basic algebra facts.

Teach Others

Teaching others is a good way to reinforce your memory of the material. It can also be a lot of fun to share the information you've learned with others. Benjamin tried this and reported, "My parents and even my annoying older brother seemed interested in what I learned about genetics. I guess my brother liked that I wasn't spending dinner time bothering him. I liked how smart I felt when I was teaching them!" You can also teach others about history, authors, or any other subject you are studying. Sometimes, if there is not a family member around, you can even teach your lesson to the family pet! When you teach the information, you may find that you need to learn more about certain areas so that you can explain the information more clearly to others.

Race Against the Clock

Another way to make homework more fun is to guess how long it will take you to do a task. Once you guess, set a timer, and see if you can beat the clock. It's important to move quickly but to also pay close attention to your work. This was really helpful for Taylor. She commented, "I like turning my math problems into a race against the clock. It makes me focus and it's like the rush of energy I need to get my work done. I make sure that I'm careful about my work so I don't make careless errors."

Create Graphic Organizers

Graphic organizers are a great way to organize your thinking before you start writing essays.

A graphic organizer is a type of picture that is used to show the connections between facts and information that you are learning. There are many different graphic organizers. They are all ways to organize your thoughts and ideas. For example, in the graphic organizer on the next page, the center circle has the main idea of Eddie's paper ("Basketball Rules"). The other circles have ideas that he wants to develop into paragraphs and they all describe details of the game. So, when Eddie sat down to write his paper, he wrote his introductory paragraph about his main idea, then used each of the other circles to form additional paragraphs. Eddie commented, "I didn't have to keep everything in my head. I just had to focus on writing one paragraph at a time. The graphic organizer helped me to be organized."

You can also search for graphic organizer apps to help you map your ideas. For example, Popplet and MindMash are two apps that help you visually organize your thoughts. You can use both text and images, which may be helpful if you are a visual learner.

Highlight Important Material

Highlighting what you read can be helpful to some people, if your teacher tells you it's okay to mark up the book. You might decide just to highlight important points in your class notes. But what do you highlight? Evan admitted, "I used to highlight everything in my books. I thought that if an author wrote something, it must be important." He later learned to highlight only key points that will help him to remember the rest of the paragraph or page. As you read, use self-talk and self-monitoring. That means that you can have a conversation with yourself and ask:

- Is this sentence important?
- What is the most important sentence in this paragraph?
- What do I need to memorize?

The answers to these questions will help you to decide what to highlight.

Take Notes

Note taking (in class when listening to your teacher or at home when reading) may cause the same potential confusion as highlighting. What's important to write down or type? Sometimes writing entire sentences is important. Sometimes an outline is enough.

Samantha used the outline form. She explained, "I put the main topic, then I listed the details instead of writing them out. So, for example, if my teacher was talking about the layers of the Earth, I listed 'Layers of Earth' on the top of the page, then used bullets to write each layer. I then added a few words about the layer. I would have never had time to write each sentence my teacher said, even if she talked slowly, which she doesn't."

You can also use graphic organizers to take notes. In the center circle, Samantha might have put "Layers of the Earth," then put each layer in one of the outer circles and listed a few details about that layer in the same circle.

Highlighting and note taking give you shortcuts for reviewing work later.

Using self-monitoring and self-talk, you can think about a lot of different ways to take notes and remember what you read. Decide what's best for you. If you are not sure, ask your friends, parents, and especially your teachers for suggestions.

Remember that you can also highlight as you review your notes. It's easier to review your work when you have certain key words or sentences jump out at you after you use a highlighter. Be careful not to use a highlighter that is too dark, since it can sometimes make reading the words more difficult.

Match Your Study Plan to the Test Format

Matching the way you study to the format of the test can help. For example, if you know that a test will have a fill-in-the-blank format, then you have to really memorize the words. You won't be reminded of them by having them on your test paper. So, if you are learning the names of Native American tribes, you really want to be able to remember those names (and how they're spelled) to fill in the blanks on the test.

If the test is multiple choice, then you just have to recognize the right words, such as the right Native American tribe, to accurately answer the question. Multiple choice tests can be tricky, though, because they may include two answers that are similar. Therefore, you want to really study how the content differs from other content studied. Imagine that you know that the answer to a question about weather is a cloud, but you aren't sure which cloud is the correct one for the test question. You are okay if the multiple choice list only gives you one kind of cloud, but usually teachers will give you more than one to test whether you really know the different types of clouds. So, for a multiple choice test, make sure to study the differences between ideas or words that you learned to make test-taking easier.

If the test is going to be an essay, practice using a graphic organizer, an outline, or another method to quickly plan a few possible essays based on the topic you are studying. You may also want to tell a family member about the test content, so you can really be sure that you can describe what you have already learned. As you read earlier, teaching the information to someone else is a great way to make sure that you understand the material and can clearly explain it!

Practice in Front of the Mirror and "Mirror" the Testing Situation

Speaking in front of the mirror can be a good way to practice giving an oral report or presentation. It may seem odd to stand in front of your mirror and present your oral report to yourself, but it often is helpful. You get to see your facial expressions and you can practice looking up from your notes and not talking too quickly.

You may also want to "mirror" (or copy) the kind of place you will take a test. For example, sit at a table rather than lie on your bed when you are practicing writing an essay. Imagine that you are sitting at your desk at school as you practice.

The more you practice for a test or presentation, and try to imitate the environment at school, the better you can prepare for the classroom situation.

Avoid Cramming

Sometimes kids (and adults!) think they can get the work done quickly, so they wait until the deadline is close. You may run out of time and feel the pressure or panic of not being able to do the kind of job you could have done with more time. You may have heard this a million times before, but be kind to yourself. Take the pressure off yourself. Knock off the assignments early so that you don't even have to think about the possible stress of cramming or running out of time to do the work.

Don't forget to reward yourself for putting in effort.

Reward Yourself!

Most people enjoy this tip. After doing work that is difficult or not your favorite thing in the world to do, try rewarding yourself. You deserve it! Even adults do this—sometimes adults will plan a fun vacation after finishing a major project at work.

Here are a few possible quick rewards to consider giving yourself:

- Five minutes listening to your favorite music
- Playing around with your pet
- Playing your favorite game for 5–10 minutes
- Working on an art project

You can also plan a bigger reward after taking a final exam or finishing a long-term project, such as going to a movie with a friend. Take a few minutes to think of how you might reward yourself. Remember to be realistic!

Creative Ways to Do Your Assignments

You may think that you have to be very serious when you study. Do you think this is what your teacher would want? Hopefully not always! There are creative and fun ways to do some of your assignments. Check with your teacher first to make sure that it's okay to use these approaches.

Create a Legal Trial

If you like debating (or arguing!), this strategy may be particularly fun for you. Examine two sides of an issue you are studying, and pretend you are a lawyer for the prosecution or defense. Megan used this approach. She said, "I was studying the conflict between America and Britain that led to America becoming an independent country. That was the exact assignment from my teacher. I got my teacher's permission, then I decided to pretend that the British put Patrick Henry on trial. I had to figure out what he would say to defend his actions and thoughts and what the British might bring up to challenge him. This wasn't easy, but it definitely was fun!" If you do this, you might end up really learning the material backwards and forwards.

School work can be fun, especially if you think creatively about it!

Become a News Reporter

There are lots of ways to use the "reporter role" while you study. Brian's English teacher asked the class to write a paper about how technology has changed the world. Brian could research the different technological advances in modern times (e.g., the fax machine, the scanner, the computer, the internet, smart phones). Perhaps he would list the dates each item was invented, how many were sold, and the new capacity that it offered to people. This may be an interesting project. But he found a more creative way to do this project.

Brian wanted to try being a news reporter and interview two fictional people—one who loves the advances in technology and talks about how each advance has benefited society and another who feels that technology is ruining society. After getting his teacher's permission, Brian typed up his pretend interviews. He later commented, "It was so much fun creating these two people and their personalities. One was a little rude and the other was busy giving stats to support his opinion. I learned a lot about the pros and cons of technology and I learned that I can be a creative writer!"

Draw Cartoons

You might be surprised to know that you can show your knowledge of a subject through cartoons. Donna's assignment was to write about the dangers of smoking and how smoking can damage your body. After checking with her teacher, she decided to use her love of art to complete this homework assignment. She explained, "I don't think that smoking is funny, so I had to be careful not to make the cartoon too funny about this serious topic. I first drew a teenager who was smoking (she had thick smoke coming out from the top of her head). Then I had her sent to the principal's office because you can't smoke at school.

"The principal had this very disapproving look on his face and talked about how cigarette smoking can hurt her. But then the principal opened some side doors in his office and people walked through with different problems from smoking. I had one man who had breathing problems and I drew him coughing all over the kid. I also drew an older woman who was crying because her husband died from smoking so much. I drew five different people. My teacher gave me an A. He never gives out As. He said that I gave him information on the effects of smoking on the body and on the people who smoke or love someone who smokes. Pretty cool, huh?"

Summary

Hopefully your tool kit is now overflowing with study tools! Have fun with the strategies and tools in this chapter. You may find that one strategy works well for a certain subject and another strategy (or combination of strategies) works better for a different subject. For example, Ken used flashcards for vocabulary and then raced against the clock for math. Try to figure out which of the senses you learn best with, and then use the strategies from the learning style section. Try not to cram. It is hard to memorize a lot of information in a short period of time. After you have worked hard, enjoy the rewards that you deserve!

8.

Skills for the Big Day at School

Before starting this chapter, take a moment to check off the skills below
that you are already comfortable using:

☐ I get rest and eat well before my big test or presentation.

☐ I use positive self-talk, deep breathing, or other strategies to stay calm
and reduce my stress on the day of my test or presentation.

☐ I read the test directions and check my answers before handing in my
test paper.

☐ I use a graphic organizer or outline to plan for essay tests, and I take
time to review my writing for grammar and spelling before turning it in.

☐ When giving a presentation in class, I don't rush, I'm organized, and
I look at people.

☐ I am clear, focused, and prepared when I talk with my teacher,
so she knows what I need.

This chapter focuses on how to handle the stress and challenges at school
when you have a big test or presentation. Some kids actually feel more
relaxed on these days, because they know that they studied hard and

prepared. All the studying, organizing, and assignments are over. Now, it's just time to show all of your work.

Many kids, though, feel some anxiety or stress on test day or presentation day. For instance, Solomon knew how to study, but he didn't know the best test-taking strategies or what to do during his class presentation to make it go well.

General Strategies for School

There are actually some helpful strategies to handle taking tests, giving presentations in class, and speaking with your teacher. In this chapter, you will learn some tips to increase your chances of success on your important day at school. These tips can also be used on other "big days," such as your sports competition or play tryout.

This chapter will also discuss some ways to fight and overcome negative self-talk and tips for sharing all your knowledge and abilities. You already learned about many ways to increase your alertness and focus when studying at home. Since most of the tips work for school as well, it's important to review them.

TOOL KIT FOR PERFORMING YOUR BEST AT SCHOOL

- Get enough sleep
- Eat a good breakfast
- Practice positive self-talk
- Remember that it's only one day
- Imagine you are just practicing
- Keep a comfort object with you
- Use your relaxation techniques from Chapter 2

Get Enough Sleep

Sometimes it's hard to fall asleep the night before a big day at school. Kim explained, "I kept going over my speech in my head and I couldn't relax and go to sleep." Bobby said he "woke up in the middle of the night and felt it was important to study again." What about you?

If sleep is a challenge before your big school day, try the relaxation exercises that you learned about in Chapter 2 to help you to relax. Plan to be done with your studying early on the night before the test or presentation. It's a night to focus more on relaxation than review. If you want to wake up a little early in the morning to review your study material, then just plan on going to sleep a little early. This way, you make sure to have enough sleep.

Eat a Good Breakfast

In addition to having a good night's sleep, try to eat breakfast on the big day. You may not want to eat. You may feel too rushed. You may feel too tense. Even if you can't eat a full meal, try eating a little bit to fuel your body. Perhaps you can bring some nutritious food to school with you, so you can eat a little more just before you enter class. Remember that food (and sleep) help your body and mind to stay alert.

Practice Positive Self-Talk

Even if you successfully battled the negative self-talk during study time, your self-doubts and negative comments about yourself may sneak back into your thinking on "game day." If you find that you are thinking, "I'm so dumb. I'll never pass this test," or "I don't know anything about this topic," try turning these negative thoughts into positive self-talk.

If you used your executive functioning skills and studied hard at home, then there are many positive statements you can say to yourself. Here are a few that have worked for other kids:

- "I studied as much as I could, so I'll just do the best I can."

- "It's okay if I don't know everything, but I think I know a lot."

- "I have my mnemonics to remind me of words for the test, so that will help."

- "I have my PowerPoint to help remind me of what to say in my presentation."

- "I can feel good that I prepared. I'm okay with how I prepared."

- "I don't have to be the best. I only have to try my best."

Remember That It's Only One Day

Sometimes the date of the test or presentation may seem like the most important day of your life. You may feel like that day will determine who you are, how smart you are, and how other people will judge you. Yikes! That's a lot of pressure!

Some teachers even focus on the test or presentation date like it is the only day in your life that will determine if you know the material. It's important for you (and your teacher!) to remember that it's only a day, just like any other day.

If you remind yourself that six months from the test date you will be focusing on other school work, other social activities, and so forth, then the one big day doesn't seem so full of pressure. No matter what, you can count on the fact that the big day will end. You will not be up in front of the class doing a presentation for years. Your test will not go on and on for months.

Focus on the good news. The test or presentation will definitely end. The test or presentation is simply a way for you to show all that you've learned.

You can feel confident, knowing that you studied and prepared.

Imagine You Are Just Practicing

In earlier chapters, you learned about ways to study and review your work. You may have even imagined taking the test or giving the presentation. If you practiced a lot, then you can "act" on the big day to decrease your tension. Act as if you are just practicing at home. Often, doing the same presentation or test at home can seem less stressful, so close your eyes for a minute, imagine you are back home, feel yourself getting calmer, then open your eyes and focus on the work.

Keep a Comfort Object With You

Wouldn't it be great to really have a magical object to help you get through your school day? I think everyone would want to buy one! Unfortunately, there is no magical object, but there are "comfort objects" that really can help. A comfort object is just something that reminds you to relax, that you are capable, or that you are cared about by others. Here are some examples:

- Gloria used the same pencil that she used when she did well on her last big test.

- Harold had a picture in his backpack showing him sailing on a boat with friends.

- Sheila had a rabbit's foot in her pocket (just a soft piece of material—not from an actual rabbit!).

Think about the comforting thoughts that you came up with in earlier chapters. Can you bring something to school and keep it in your backpack or pocket to look at or touch to remind you of relaxing moments in your life? It may decrease the stress you feel just before your test or presentation.

Use Your Relaxation Techniques

If you expect to feel stress on the big day at school, then try using some of the other strategies from Chapter 2 that helped you relax at home. They may include:

- Deep breathing
- Practicing progressive muscle relaxation
- Shaking and relaxing
- Imagining success

- Seeking out a support person in school before the test or presentation
- Counting

Test Day Success Strategies

If you have been studying, you don't need to learn new material on the day of your test. However, there are some things that you can do before the test to increase the chances that you will do your best.

Read the Directions Carefully

Sometimes, when you are nervous or anxious to get the test done, the directions may seem obvious. You may just read them quickly. Andy thought he read the test directions. He explained, "I thought I read the directions carefully for my multiple choice test. I thought the directions said that I should circle the right answer for each question." Andy thought the test was hard, since he often felt torn between two answers. If he had read the actual directions, he was supposed to circle the *two* right answers for each question. Andy was not happy with his grade.

TOOL KIT FOR TEST SUCCESS

- **Read the directions carefully**
- **Check your answers**
- **Use the process of elimination**
- **Skip challenging questions**
- **Use your study techniques**

Andy's error is not that unusual. For example, your math teacher may ask that you show your work. If you do not read the directions, and you get the right answer without showing your work, you may not get full credit for your answer. After all of your studying, it's important to get the grade you deserve. Following the directions carefully gives you a better chance of getting credit for all the work you've done.

Check Your Answers

Have you ever heard the expression "two heads are better than one"? The idea is that having two people brainstorm an answer may lead to a more accurate answer. Since you usually can't team up with a friend to take the test, you can rely on yourself to have "two heads."

How is this possible? Well, you can first be the test taker and then be the answer checker. First, do your best and take the test. Then, catch your breath and use one of the relaxation techniques from Chapter 2 to relax. Once you've had a chance to calm yourself and clear your head, check your answers. Checking answers is a great strategy to catch careless errors and make sure you answered the question.

Use the Process of Elimination

If you are taking a matching or multiple-choice test, make sure to find out beforehand if you lose points for making educated guesses. If no points are taken off for making guesses, then a great strategy to use is the "process of elimination."

Let's say you have four choices for answering the question. You know that one choice is totally wrong. Cross it out. You know that another choice is almost definitely wrong. Cross that out. That leaves two answers that may be right. If you don't get points off for guessing, then take a guess between the remaining two answers—you have a 50 percent chance of getting it right!

Skip Challenging Questions

If you get stuck on a test question, but think you might know the answer, skip it, finish the test, then go back to the challenging question. When the rest of the test is done, you may be able to spend more time on this question without feeling like you'll never get to the rest of the test. It can be helpful to put a star or circle next to the question, so you can find it later. Before doing this, though, it's important to know whether your teacher would allow you to go back and answer questions on other pages of the test booklet. Find out this information before starting the test.

Use Your Study Techniques

If you used mnemonics to study, see if your teacher will let you scribble them at the top of your paper so that you have them handy. If not, then just remember to think back to the study tricks you used so that you focus on them to help you on test day.

Essay Test Success Strategies

The test is not the time to just start writing, then add facts, then write an introduction. Your teacher is probably hoping for an essay that is organized and communicates the answer to the essay question. Here are a few tips:

TOOL KIT FOR ESSAY TEST SUCCESS

- **Read the question carefully**
- **Use a graphic organizer or outline**
- **Don't assume your teacher understands what you mean**
- **Watch the clock**
- **Review your work**

Read the Question Carefully

Just as you must read the instructions on your other tests, you should read the essay question carefully to make sure your essay addresses it. It can be easy to get sidetracked once you start your essay. Pause a couple of times to re-read the question and make sure you are answering it.

Use a Graphic Organizer or Outline

If you are allowed, use a graphic organizer before starting to write so you know what you are going to write about and in what order. If you don't like graphic organizers, simply outline what you will write before you start.

Don't Assume Your Teacher Understands What You Mean

Pretend you are writing for a reader who doesn't know the material. This will help you make sure that your writing is clear.

Watch the Clock

If you have several essays, think about how much time you have and figure out how much time you can spend on each essay. Allow yourself a few minutes to review your work. Then watch the clock to make sure you don't run out of time.

Review Your Work

After finishing the test, try to find some time to review what you wrote and edit sections that are unclear or don't make sense. You might be surprised that you wrote something slightly different than what you were thinking.

Also, even though you were focused on answering the question, teachers usually care about your spelling and handwriting too. Keep this in mind as you write, and try to fix spelling errors or messy handwriting when you're finished.

Presentation or Oral Report Day Success Strategies

Do you ever get nervous before speaking in front of your class? You are not alone! It's very common to be nervous about public speaking. Thankfully, there are some great tips for giving a clear, interesting presentation in class. In fact, there are some people who go all over America teaching the strategies for speaking in front of groups. This section covers a few pointers that you might find useful.

Use Visual Aids

Some kids love when everyone in the class looks at them and listens to what they are saying. For other kids, this is the worst part of giving a presentation in class. Many kids are a little self-conscious when everyone looks at them.

There are some creative tools that you can use when you give oral reports so that everyone in the class can look at something other than you. Ryan uses PowerPoint presentations as his "assistant" in class. He reported, "I love PowerPoint. I don't need to use index cards to keep organized, because each PowerPoint slide is like a note card,

TOOL KIT FOR GIVING PRESENTATIONS

- Use visual aids
- Take your time
- Look people in the eyes
- Tell jokes, if the topic allows for it
- Be organized
- Don't fear other kids' reactions
- Practice thought stopping

reminding me of what I want to talk about. I also notice that most of the kids, and even the teacher, look at the PowerPoint a lot. This way, I feel more comfortable because they're not staring at me!"

Think about what kind of tools you can use to keep everyone focused on your topic, but also allow them to look or listen to something other than you. Just check with your teacher to make sure that your ideas are acceptable in the class and for the assignment. Here are a few ideas:

- Use a large poster with a timeline or pictures of the person you are talking about.

- With the help of friends, videotape a play or presentation displaying what you learned about the topic.

- Use PowerPoint slides to outline your presentation or highlight important points.

Take Your Time

Some kids try to race through their presentation to get it over with as fast as possible. They try to talk quickly and say as much as they can before they gasp for air. This kind of talking and breathing will not keep you calm and relaxed.

Before you stand up to do your presentation, take a few moments to focus on positive self-talk (e.g., "I don't have to be perfect. I know what I'm talking about so I just have to talk about it") and ways to relax. A common technique is to imagine your audience in their underwear. How judgmental could they be if they were at school in their underwear! Try to remind yourself that you will probably judge yourself more harshly than others will.

If you feel confident that you practiced the presentation enough at home, and have a plan to present it in an organized manner, then it's just "show time." You may feel a little excitement and anxiety. This is normal. If you slowly walk to the front of the room, take a deep breath, and take a few seconds to look around the room and smile at everyone (you can even say "hi!"), you may be able to convince yourself that you are not on trial. You are just sharing your knowledge with other people who may not have studied your topic.

Look People in the Eyes

You certainly don't need to stare at everyone while you talk. In fact, for many presentations, your teacher would be pleased to know that you have note cards or an outline to refer to during your speech. Looking at the people in the audience, though, is sometimes important, so they feel recognized and so you keep their attention. If you talk to the floor, they may feel like you aren't talking to them. They might daydream. Making eye contact is actually a way to help your classmates (and teacher) stay focused on your report.

Tell Jokes, If the Topic Allows for It

Sometimes teachers may feel that a student is not taking the presentation seriously if there are a lot of jokes in the speech. On the other hand, sometimes teachers or kids may feel that the topic isn't interesting without a joke or two. Think about your personality, whether you are comfortable joking, and whether the topic allows for humor. If you are talking about a tragedy, joking is probably not going to fit into your discussion. If you are giving a book report, you might be able to make a quick joke about how you identified with a funny action by one of the characters, or how you enjoyed the author's sarcastic description.

Be Organized

One of the easiest ways to confuse your audience is to jump from one topic to another, then back again. Making sure that you are organized can help stop this from happening. Lilly said, "I noticed other kids looking away from me and they stopped taking notes when I was giving my report. I asked my best friend what happened and she said that she didn't know what I was talking about because I kept saying

KIDS' QUESTIONS ANSWERED!

Adam's Question: **I think I'm the class nerd. I really like studying and doing great on tests. I know some kids think I'm weird. What should I say to them?**

Adam, it's hard to know how other people really feel about you unless you ask or they tell you. Are kids really judging you negatively? There are other possibilities, such as:

- They think you are "weird smart" and it's a compliment.

- They are jealous of your ability to do well in school.

- They don't know how else to relate to you, other than to label you.

- They question their own skills when they're around you.

Before focusing on the other kids, think about your internal judgment of yourself. You mentioned that you think you are a "class nerd." Are you okay with this image?

    If you like who you are but want to be accepted by other kids, you might try:

- finding out about what other kids like and talking with them about these interests sometimes.

- balancing studying with hanging with friends.

If you really only want to know what to say to kids about your study habits, here are some lines that may be helpful:

- "I don't always love studying everything. But I want to get good grades, so I do it anyway."

- "I have a system for homework that works. Want me to share it with you?"

Remember that you don't need to apologize for who you are. After all, you are not hurting anyone and you are just trying to take school work seriously.

'he' but she wasn't sure which 'he' since I was talking about a bunch of scientists. I was also talking about their discoveries and then talking about the scientists again and people lost track of what scientist made which discovery."

Note cards, PowerPoint slides, and outlines are a great way to keep organized. Writing key points on the board can also allow kids to focus on the highlights of your presentation. Mnemonics can also be useful to make sure that you remember all the material that you need to present. (See Chapter 7 for some popular mnemonic devices.)

> **When giving a speech, it is time for you to teach, not time for others to judge you.**

Don't Fear Other Kids' Reactions

There are some kids who fear being laughed at or made fun of when they are giving a speech. While there is no guarantee that this won't happen at times, many kids will be supportive, since they know that they have to give presentations as well.

If someone does laugh at you or make faces while you are talking, here are some tips:

- Don't look at that person, so his faces won't bother or distract you.

- Pick out a few supportive listeners to look at during your speech.

- Remember that just because someone is laughing doesn't mean there is something wrong with you (positive self-talk).

- If the student is very disruptive and you feel you can't continue, you can ask him (calmly) if he has a question for you so that you can help him understand your lesson. Just make sure your question doesn't seem like a confrontation or like you want to start a fight with him.

- Focus on how much you prepared and how much you have to share with the class.

- Talk to the teacher after the lesson ends.

Practice Thought Stopping

Sometimes other thoughts can interrupt your focus when you are giving a presentation. For instance, you may think about whether you will get a good or bad grade. If you put in the work, planned out what you wanted to say, and shared your ideas with your teacher beforehand, then you don't really need to think about your grade at the moment of your presentation. You may worry about whether other kids will find the speech interesting. Or you may all of a sudden think about a test that is going to happen the next day or play tryouts that afternoon.

There is a technique called "thought stopping." It's easy to understand, but not instantly easy to do. However, you can get the hang of it with some practice. You just think, "Stop!" and decide on a better time to think about that topic. So if you are in the middle of a presentation and are thinking, "I wonder how this is going. I really want an A," say to yourself, "Stop! I will think about it later. Now, I'll focus on the presentation." You may even want to write the thought down on a piece of paper if it's likely to interfere when you are talking to the class. That way, it is out of your head and on the paper before you even start giving your presentation!

Speaking With Your Teacher

You may find that you get nervous when speaking to your teacher outside of class. Some kids enjoy talking with their teachers, some kids get nervous talking to any teacher, and other kids get nervous only when talking to certain teachers. If you feel uncomfortable when talking with your teacher, you are certainly not the first student to feel this way.

The strategies that you read about earlier in this chapter might help you here. Think about decreasing negative self-talk. If you think that your teacher will get

Remember that you don't have to get 100 or give the best presentation ever—just work to make yourself proud!

annoyed if you ask for some extra help, investigate whether this might be the wrong conclusion. You could ask other kids if they have ever received extra help from this teacher. You can even ask the teacher how he or she suggests that you get extra help. Communicating with your teacher is important. If you go for extra help at a time of day when your teacher is running to a meeting, you may not get the warm reception you were hoping to receive.

Your teacher may also respond with a bit of frustration if you go for extra help and ask him to reteach the entire lesson. It can be quite useful to tell your teacher what parts of the lesson you didn't understand and what specific questions you have. This shows that you cared enough to think about the material.

Plan what you want to say to your teacher and what your goal would be for the discussion. This way, you can get right to the point and, hopefully, begin getting the help you need quickly.

Summary

In this chapter, you read about how to get through the "big day." You learned strategies for taking a test, giving a speech in class, and talking with your teacher outside of the classroom. Now you have some skills to get through your tests and presentations with confidence, and show off everything you've learned!

Conclusion

From now on, when you are sitting in class or when you are doing your homework, remember that you have an entire tool kit filled with ways to manage academic stress and strategies to help you do your work.

Here are a few reminders:

- Figuring out what causes you stress is the first step toward reducing it.
- You learned about ways to calm yourself down and relax.
- Even if you can't change the situation that is causing you stress, you can change the way you think about it.
- Organization takes a little time to do, but disorganization takes a lot of time to repair.
- Remember that executive functioning skills can help you get through your work.
- You can be creative in having a social life while still getting your work done.
- There are ways to make studying easier and more fun.
- You can feel confident on test day, knowing that you studied hard and prepared.

And, finally, keep in mind that you had the courage to go through this book and learn new skills. School is similar to this. You learn new skills each day. Ask questions when you need help and try to enjoy the journey! It really can be enjoyable!

About the Authors

Wendy L. Moss, PhD, ABPP, FAASP, has her doctorate in clinical psychology, is a licensed psychologist, and has a certification in school psychology. Dr. Moss has practiced in the field of psychology for over 30 years and has worked in hospital, residential, private practice, clinic, and school settings.

She has the distinction of being recognized as a diplomate in school psychology by the American Board of Professional Psychology for her advanced level of competence in the field of school psychology. Dr. Moss has been appointed as a fellow in the American Academy of School Psychology.

In addition, she is the author of *Being Me: A Kid's Guide to Boosting Confidence and Self-Esteem* and *Children Don't Come With an Instruction Manual: A Teacher's Guide to Problems That Affect Learners,* and has written several articles. Dr. Moss is currently an ad hoc reviewer for the *Journal for Specialists in Group Work* and the *Journal of School Psychology.*

Robin A. DeLuca-Acconi, LCSW, is a licensed clinical social worker, and has a certification in school social work. Ms. Acconi has practiced in the field of social work for almost 15 years and has worked in schools, youth, community, and family counseling agencies.

She has been a parent educator and staff trainer, conducting workshops on anxiety and stress reduction, conflict management, social skills, and optimizing executive functioning skills. She has authored pamphlets and manuals on social and emotional learning and friendship development. In addition, she has presented for national and international audiences on "Awakening the Global Consciousness of Students" and "Teaching for Peace and Human Rights." She is currently pursuing her doctorate in social work policy.